A SINGULAR
LIFE™

Secrets to living well

with or without

a traditional partner

Greta Booth

ISBN 979-8-9993853-3-8
ISBN 979-8-9993853-1-4 (ebook)

Remember – Greta Booth isn't your therapist! But for more stories, secrets, and recommendations from the author, sign up for her free newsletter at asingularlife.com or follow @asingularlifebook on social media.

DEDICATION

I dedicate this book to my parents – my father, the ultimate
Good Guy, and my mother, a truly Singular Woman – whose
love and patience enabled me to discover how to live well
with or without a traditional partner.

CONTENTS

```
sin-gu-lar
adjective
1. referring to only one person or thing
2. remarkably good or great; extraordinary
```

1. INTRODUCTION

If you are reading this, chances are that you are single – or you're about to be. Or maybe you're in a relationship but you are single-curious. Perhaps you are content in your romantic relationship, but sense that something else is lacking in your life.

Many books geared towards single people, especially single women, try to "help them" to no longer be single. *The Rules: Time-tested Secrets for Capturing the Heart of Mr. Right*,[1] *Why Men Love Bitches*,[2] and *Act Like a Lady, Think Like a Man*[3] are some classics that many women have read at one point or another in an effort to maneuver their way into a romantic relationship.

Not this book. The goal of this book is to help women build rich, fulfilling lives with or without a partner, and to be able to walk away and take care of themselves should a relationship ultimately sour. Because the fact is, many relationships will.

---

[1] Ellen Fein and Sherri Schneider, *The Rules: Time-tested Secrets for Capturing the Heart of Mr. Right* (Grand Central Publishing, 2007).

[2] Sherry Argov, *Why Men Love Bitches: From Doormat to Dreamgirl—A Woman's Guide to Holding Her Own in a Relationship* (Adams Media, 2002).

[3] Steve Harvey, *Act Like a Lady, Think Like a Man, Expanded Edition: What Men Really Think About Love, Relationships, Intimacy, and Commitment—Relationship Advice from a Man's Perspective* (Amistad, 2014).

A more similar comparison to this book, and a major source of inspiration, would be Helen Gurley Brown's iconic *Sex and the Single Girl*,[4] not to be confused with Candace Bushnell's *Sex and the City*[5] (although that is of course a classic, as well). Gurley Brown's book, however, served as a sort of retro "how-to" book that helped women of the 1960s navigate being single and support themselves financially. However, it still ultimately sought to get single women wedding proposals; and the advice, while at times hilarious, is quite dated.

While the book you're holding in your hands is indeed a how-to guide on how to successfully be single, my goal is far different: I'm striving to help you find happiness on your own and to make yourself so self-sufficient financially, physically, and emotionally that until you meet a romantic partner who adds value to your life, you will be better off staying single.

What do I mean by "value"? Not money, for one thing – at least for me. As I will explain in Chapter 7, I have learned the hard way to never date anybody purely for financial reasons. But everyone has to figure out for themselves what "value" means in a relationship.

The truth is that women inherently bring a lot of value into relationships, but they are often better off being alone until they find someone who provides at least some kind of value of their own.

Better off being alone, you might ask? But the world is designed for couples, isn't it? It sure is. Rent and mortgage are so much easier to pay when you're splitting them down the middle, as well as other household bills. Married people

---

[4] Helen Gurley Brown, *Sex and the Single Girl* (Barricade Books, 2003).
[5] Candace Bushnell, *Sex and the City* (Grove Press, 2011).

also get a tax break – as well as a wide host of household gifts and money at their wedding, setting them up with a solid foundation for early adulthood.

People in romantic relationships often seem to get a 50 percent discount in life. This book strives to help the single folk out by taking the pressure off in finding a lifelong mate. It offers stories, tips, and examples of how to optimize your income, take care of your health, build strong community ties, and otherwise enjoy your life – with or without someone by your side.

This book is also not necessarily only for single *women*, but as a single straight woman myself, it is written from that specific perspective. But there are lessons in here that I certainly hope could help people of any gender or sexual identity. I even welcome straight men to read it if they want to gain insight into the female perspective.

And finally, this book is for those of all ages, but for reasons that will soon be apparent, the sooner it gets into their hands the better.

Being single can be a wonderful thing.

"Really?" you might be thinking. *"How?"* For starters, being single means that you are not in a bad or abusive intimate relationship. According to the National Domestic Violence Hotline,[6] about one in four women and one in seven men have experienced physical violence by their intimate partner sometime in their lifetimes, and it can be incredibly difficult to leave these relationships.

Furthermore, almost *half* of all women and men in

---

[6] "Domestic Violence Statistics," National Domestic Violence Hotline, last accessed June 13, 2025, https://www.thehotline.org/stakeholders/domestic-violence-statistics/.

the US have experienced psychological aggression by an intimate partner (this author is one of them).

In addition, being single means that you are not wasting time in an unfulfilling or non-reciprocal intimate relationship, a relationship you may have ended up in because you feared being alone or wanted to prove to society that you're worthy of "being picked." This could be a relationship which depletes your time and energy without imparting any real kind of benefit.

Of course, being single also means that you are not currently in a "good" romantic relationship with another person. Yes, I do believe good romantic relationships – and Good Guys – exist. My parents have a healthy, if imperfect relationship, as do my siblings and some close friends and colleagues. I have experienced some, as well.

How do I define a "good relationship"? I personally define one as "good" where there is a somewhat balanced give-and-take of energy and resources, and loving, honest communication. The energy exchange may not be 50-50 all the time – sometimes it might be 60-40, or in tough times, even 90-10 – but over time, it should balance out, or at least be at a level both parties are satisfied with.

However, this book is not about the good relationships. It's about how to pick yourself up after a bad one, or after a period of being unhappily single. It's about taking concrete steps towards making your life better than it was before – without having it "center" around someone else, as a growing chorus of single women are saying on social media. It's about requiring the next person you date to add some kind of value to your life, and to not just take, take, take – whether it's your time, money, or energy.

Enjoying being single right now does not mean you cannot experience a good relationship in the future. In fact, it can make you an immensely better, more interesting partner in the long run and, at the very least, help create a more fulfilling relationship with yourself.

When something just feels off

If you are single, or were single for a long time, chances are that you are pretty smart. A 2012 study[7] found a number of connections between those with high intelligence and staying single, including their tendency to remain single longer than their peers.

Smart people are perhaps less inclined to conform to societal expectations like getting married if something in the relationship just feels off. Believe me, I personally spent many years dating, in relationships, and scrolling on dating apps because I felt so much pressure from the world to get married, or to at least be in a relationship. I have also observed other women in their 20s and early 30s prematurely *lose their hair* over the stress and stigma of being single. Had most of us simply lowered our standards, yes, we could be married and have kept all of our hair. But would we be *happy*? Most likely not – and we were smart enough to discern the difference.

Women of the Gen X and millennial generations have especially been victim to this unfair expectation. We were raised on fairy tales and Disney movies where the only possible ending was being saved by a prince and falling in love. In fact, an older work colleague once told me that if you didn't get married by age 30 in the 1980s or 90s, it was widely

[7] Pieternel Dijkstra et al., "Personality and Well-being: Do the Intellectually Gifted Differ From the General Population?" Advanced Development 13 (2012), last accessed June 13, 2025,
https://www.proquest.com/openview/e3172a3e4f5fb6de3b69bb39925f9abf/1?pq-origsite=gscholar&cbl=28640.

5

accepted that there was something wrong with you.

Over the years, we as a society have become a bit more evolved and it's no longer as shocking to stay single into your 30s and beyond. As *Psychology Today* reports,[8] Gen Z in particular doesn't seem to judge their peers as much for staying single.

But a certain level of self-consciousness among single women remains. We're still in a society where some loud voices try to shame "single cat ladies" or women who, for a wide variety of reasons, have chosen to be single. Single men have, of course, not faced nearly the same level of public derision or judgement, if at all.

Who am I to talk, anyway?

Before we go any further, let me tell you a bit about myself. I am not an official "dating expert" by any means – but is anyone, really? However, I *am* a 41-year-old woman who has spent the past 25 years dating, in relationships, breaking up, scrolling on dating apps, and being single. I have dated lots of men and it has never felt right to marry any of them – even those with whom I was in "good" relationships (and there have been several). I do not feel like any one of them is "the one that got away."

Over the past 20 or so years, I am fortunate enough to have had a variety of family members, professional mentors, and just generally people wiser than myself help guide me as I've embarked into adulthood. I've learned so much from them in terms of building a foundation for robust finances, good health, and a supportive community. And I am lucky to

---

[8] August Brunsman, "Why Gen Zers Are Single—and Happy About It," Psychology Today, August 2024, last accessed June 13, 2025, https://www.psychologytoday.com/us/blog/talking-apes/202408/why-gen-zers-are-single-and-happy-about-it.

have had the freedom to further experiment on my own in creating a fulfilling life and to learn through (much) trial and error.

Recently, while relaxing in my beautiful, peaceful home (more on this later), I experienced the revelation that I have been happiest and most myself when I am single and not looking. While I would certainly consider a romantic relationship with the right person should he come along, he would have to make my life even better than it is now for the relationship to be worth it – and my life is pretty damn good.

Someone who adds value to *my* life would be someone who offers kindness, emotional support, laughter, and a lot of fun. Someone who can support himself and who works hard to help support his loved ones, whether they be children, elderly parents, or, eventually, me. Someone who wants to care for me emotionally and in little ways, whether bringing me coffee, making fun plans, or sending me memes.

I tell a lot of different stories in this book, and yes, many are directly related to dating. But many stories are not about dating, or men, at all. They're about *living* – particularly about how to live well.

These stories mostly involve me and my own experiences, but there are also some about the experiences of my friends. In every story, I have changed the names of all parties involved, as well as details that may identify them, in an effort to protect their privacy – as well as myself from their wrath. In certain instances, I have also shortened timelines of events and condensed conversations for the sake of brevity and smooth storytelling. However, the essence of each story, as well as each lesson, remains the same.

2. IS MARRIAGE A TRICK?

From bridal dolls to romantic comedies, women in older generations seem to have been groomed from early childhood to make their wedding day the highlight of their existence. But how many women go through the painstaking wedding preparations, hold a beautiful ceremony, go on their honeymoon, and upon their return, realize they have no idea what they got themselves into?

Women have long been told that men don't want to commit, that marriage is a drag for them, that men don't want a "ball and chain" waiting for them at home every night. And sure, there are some men who do feel that way. But many men *do* want to get married – because as author Dr. Venus Nicolino has noted on podcasts like *Uncut and Uncensored*,[9] marriage is not only designed *for* men – it's designed *by* them.

Do you think men would have created marriage in the first place, thousands of years ago, if there wasn't anything in it for them? Yes, it was often a business arrangement among the wealthy, but poorer couples got

---

[9] Caroline Stanbury, "Why Marriage Doesn't Work for Women! With special guest Dr. Venus Nicolino," Uncut and Uncensored with Caroline Stanbury, episode 99, Dear Media, 46 minutes, July 6, 2022, https://podcasts.apple.com/cy/podcast/why-marriage-doesnt-work-for-women-with-special-guest/id1524317541?i=1000568977776.

married, too.

According to Dr. Nicolino, a study conducted from the 1970s to the 2020s shows that married men have more sex than single men, live longer, report a higher quality of life, and report making more money.

But does their happiness come at a cost to their wives? Because conversely, since the 1970s, married women have been reported to die sooner than single women, experience a lower quality of life, experience a lower quality of sex, and make less money.

Single women with no kids, on the other hand, have been reported to be "the happiest subset of humans on the goddamn planet," according to Dr. Nicolino.

And yet, society has succeeded in making women feel like it's *they* who are the lucky ones to get a guy to commit to them for the rest of their lives. And many women are so blinded by the excitement and beauty of the wedding day and a vision of love and a white picket-fence that they do not clearly perceive what their marriage will look like on the other side.

Beyond the wedding day

There are certainly great, solid relationships and marriages out there. But with roughly half of marriages ending in divorce, there are clearly ones that are not so great. And often, women cite an inequal distribution of household labor as the cause for divorce.

According to American Survey Center,[10] research shows that as of 2023, married women still do a

---

[10] Daniel A. Cox, "Is Marriage Better for Men?" American Survey Center, November 30, 2023, last accessed June 13, 2025,
https://www.americansurveycenter.org/newsletter/is-marriage-better-for-men/#.

disproportionate amount of household work, whether it's laundry, cooking, or cleaning. The disparity grows worse among those who are parents. The survey found that mothers are far more involved in scheduling playdates and making medical decisions for their children. The only area where men did more than women was home repair and yard work.

New York Times reporter Claire Cain Miller[11] found that even young men who welcome gender equality are doing far less work around the house than their wives. So as young women invest more time and money in their education and professional endeavors, there is much more at stake.

I have witnessed such a dynamic first-hand. A friend of a friend, we'll call her Katie, married a super progressive, seemingly open-minded guy we will call Chris. I only met Chris once, and liked him a lot, but I was shocked to later learn about his backward views on domestic chores. Apparently when Katie and Chris were preparing to host a birthday party for their two-year-old son, and Katie was eight months pregnant, she wanted to hire a cleaning service to prepare their house for guests, several of whom were staying overnight. Chris did not like that at all. He said that, to his knowledge, his female relatives never hired anyone to clean their homes and hiring someone else to do it just seemed off.

Poor Katie almost started to cry. She was still working full-time at this point and could literally be giving birth at any moment. She was sweating buckets daily in their un-air-conditioned house in the late summer heat, and she was experiencing great general discomfort. She asked Chris if he was planning to clean the house himself, despite already

[11] Claire Cain Miller, "Young men embrace gender equality, but they still don't vacuum," *New York Times*, February 11, 2020, https://www.nytimes.com/2020/02/11/upshot/gender-roles-housework.html.

knowing the answer. He looked surprised at the question and offered a half-hearted attempt to help.

Many men of the Gen X and millennial generations love to remember how their mothers ran their households growing up and always had dinner on the table. But they fail to remember that their mothers often did not have nine-to-five jobs. These days and in this economy, it is much harder for women to stay home and focus on the house and family – although many would love to do so. They are still expected to work full-time jobs *and* complete the vast majority of the household labor. This expectation is one of the leading factors of divorce.

In a study[12] conducted by Lucia Ciciolla and Suniya S. Luthar which focused on mostly upper-middle class married women with children, most of the women were again responsible for handling the schedules of children and maintaining the home. On the other hand, however, responsibility was still largely shared between the wife and husband to financially support the family. Feeling disproportionately responsible for household management, especially care of the children, seemed to put a strain on the women's personal well-being as well as lower satisfaction with their relationship with their husbands.

In other words, in many marriages these days, both spouses are required to work full-time to earn enough money to support their families, but women are still expected to do most of the household labor – as well as give their bodies to men on a regular basis.

Many women have walked down the aisle only to

---

[12] Lucia Ciciolla and Suniya S. Luthar, "Invisible Household Labor and Ramifications for Adjustment: Mothers as Captains of Households," Sex Roles 81, 467–486 (2019), last accessed June 13, 2025, https://link.springer.com/article/10.1007/s11199-018-1001-x.

realize these expectations after the wedding day. Is that why women are initiating more divorces than men? According to American Survey Center,[13] among straight women, 66 percent say they made the decision to end their marriages while only 39 percent of divorced men said the same.

A Pew study[14] found that men are also more likely than women to remarry after a marriage ends. Is that because men realize how good they have it in a marriage? Men get to die first, statistically speaking, while having someone else do their household labor until the end?

With that said, there *are* men out there, unlike our friend Chris, who gladly agree to hire regular household cleaning services to make the domestic load more equal, or even help do it themselves. But until you find a man like that, you may want to ask yourself if you would be better off single.

Marriage scare tactics

As many women can attest, years ago women were often made to feel "less than" if they didn't get married. Was the propagation of the "old spinster" and "crazy cat lady" a scare tactic to get women to sign up for a life of servitude? Arguably, this still happens now, although hopefully less often.

Even well-meaning family and friends can often try to scare you in an effort to get you married. Common concerns include that they don't want you "to die alone," "be alone for

[13] Daniel A. Cox, "Is Marriage Better for Men?" American Survey Center, November 30, 2023, last accessed June 13, 2025,
https://www.americansurveycenter.org/newsletter/is-marriage-better-for-men/#.
[14] Gretchen Livingston, "Four-in-Ten Couples are Saying 'I Do,' Again," Pew Research Center, November 14, 2014, last accessed June 13, 2025,
https://www.pewresearch.org/social-trends/2014/11/14/chapter-2-the-demographics-of-remarriage/.

the holidays," or "be alone for the rest of your life." Let's take a moment to really examine these fears head-on and dismantle them one by one.

"We don't want you to die alone."

I have news for the people who say this to single women: on average, men usually die first. Harvard reported in 2023[15] that this death gap is widening, with American men dying nearly six years before women.

So while it might make sense for men to marry so they don't die alone – provided they don't get divorced – it does not make sense for women to make this fear-based decision.

Some might counter that married women often have children who will be there for them until they die. People who work in nursing homes might tell you differently. I once joked to a group of people at a party that I wanted to have kids just so I have someone to take care of me when I'm older. It turned out someone in the group worked in a nursing home. She said that many of the patients there have kids who never come visit them at all.

This is anecdotal information of course, and there isn't much data on nursing home visits that I could find. (Maybe there is a reason for that.) But ultimately, I do not think our marital status will dictate when, where, or how we die.

The truth is that death will most likely not be fun, no matter what. I personally would rather enjoy the vast majority of my life and peace out alone than spend my life

---

[15] "U.S. men die nearly six years before women, as life expectancy gap widens," Harvard T.H. Chan School of Public Health, November 13, 2023, last accessed June 13, 2025, https://hsph.harvard.edu/news/u-s-men-die-nearly-six-years-before-women-as-life-expectancy-gap-widens/.

struggling in a bad or mediocre marriage, take care of my husband while *he* dies, and then still die alone myself.

"Do you want to spend the holidays alone?"

The fear of spending holidays alone is also an irrationally powerful one. Who hasn't romanticized the thought of a cozy Thanksgiving or Christmas cuddling with a loved one before a fire or holiday tree?

The holidays are often over-romanticized in movies and social media, so don't for a second believe that all couples are having a picture-perfect, lovey-dovey holiday experience. Having a spouse and kids can actually make the holidays far more expensive and stressful. Many married women can't wait for them to be over. Count your blessings.

Second, just because you're single does not mean you will be celebrating alone. That's what extended family and friends are for. Nuclear families often want to make their own holidays more special by celebrating them with relatives. Nurture your relationships with parents and siblings if you can. Be the fun aunt or uncle that nieces and nephews love to see during the holidays.

If you don't have extended family (or one you *want* to spend the holidays with), take the initiative and host a holiday gathering yourself, inviting other single friends, colleagues, and your least annoying married friends. Create new traditions.

You could also seize the opportunity to take an amazing trip or create your own special solo rituals. (Eat as much pumpkin pie as you want! Watch a documentary on how a married woman faked her death to escape her family. Or just pretend it's a normal day.)

Even if you're completely miserable and depressed on the days of Thanksgiving, Christmas, Hannukah, or whatever holidays you celebrate, those are just a few days of the year. Wouldn't you rather be alone for 1-3 days of the year than in a bad relationship for 365?

"Do you want to be alone for the rest of your life?"

If you do things right, you might just want to! If you follow the tenets of the rest of this book, it is at least very likely that no one will ever feel sorry for you for being single again. In fact, as Helen Gurley Brown once said, many married women will likely envy you – for your free time, disposable income, and total freedom over how you spend both.

So take a break from scrolling the dating apps and focus on building yourself a singular life instead. If the right man comes along, wonderful. But if he doesn't, you could be living so well that you won't even care.

3. TAKE THE PRESSURE OFF

I can still remember lying on my bed when I was about 29 years old, having a near panic attack because my latest relationship didn't work out. *How many child-bearing years do I have left?* I wondered. This was before freezing my eggs was an option, and my brain was in a frenzy trying to calculate the number of years I had before I would have to turn to IVF, and what that meant for my timeline of dating, getting engaged, and marriage. *What if I'm not engaged, or even have a boyfriend, by 35?*

Suddenly, I remembered a conversation I had with my mother when I was around the age of six or seven. She was complaining once again about how she felt like she was "everybody's maid"– with "everybody" meaning everybody in our six-person household. She cooked all our meals, packed our lunches, did everyone's laundry, cleaned the house, pinched pennies every way she could, and drove me and my three siblings to all our activities and play dates while my father worked full-time. My mother rarely had a moment – or dollar – to spend on herself. Even at my young age, I could see the toll it was taking on her. *Imagine what it's like for mothers who also have to work full-time!*

"I never want to have kids," I announced. My mother

looked at me, surprised.

"Don't say that," she scolded me. "Of course you want to have kids."

Huh? Needless to say, it was confusing for me as a young child how these words so blatantly conflicted with my mother's sentiments. Of course she loved us and was glad she had us (I hope), but life seemed so hard for her day in and day out.

But my mother's reaction was just one example of how we collectively as a society convince women, even and especially as young girls, that "of course we want kids" when the reality of having them can be so taxing.

Recalling this conversation at age 29, while lying on my bed, I wondered for the first time since that moment if I really even *wanted* kids. Why was I putting so much pressure on myself? Was it to just meet society's expectations, so no one would think there was "Something Wrong" with me? What if I just... didn't have kids? Would the world end?

Or, what if I at least stopped stressing myself out over it? If I had kids, cool (I guess), but if not, there were definite advantages to not having them and another kind of life out there. Isn't what is meant to be, will be?

I recommend that every woman consider if she really wants children or if she has been programmed to think she does. Spend time with married friends or family members with kids and observe their lives. Ask yourself if you can even afford to have kids, because they are incredibly expensive. If this is still what you want, these days there are so many ways to take power into your own hands without forcing a bad relationship. You can freeze your eggs, consider fostering or adopting a child, or decide to start small and get a dog instead.

As I lay on my bed in that moment, I decided to surrender total control of whether I would have kids to the universe. Whatever would be would have to fucking be. And in doing this, I could literally feel the muscles in my neck, shoulders, and stomach relax and the tension leave my body. My body melted into the mattress. The surrender was completely liberating.

Women put pressure on themselves in other ways, as well, and it doesn't necessarily end for those who *do* get married. The pressure to be a good mom, to earn money, to stay in shape, to provide enough sex to their husband, to cook for their family, to keep a clean house — often while wondering if their man has a wandering eye. To me, being married or in domestic partnership seems like a game that can be nearly impossible to win – even if you do marry a Good Guy. As much as I love my girlfriends' husbands and partners (most of them, at least), I would not trade places with 95 percent of my girlfriends because I see all the stress they're under.

The numbers are not in women's favor either. In a now-infamous viral post on social media, Scott Galloway of the *Prof G Pod* podcast reported that if there were 50 guys and 50 women on a dating app, 46 of the women would be vying for the same four guys. That basically means that those four guys can metaphorically get away with murder in their relationships. If they behave badly and get broken up with, they literally have a queue of women eager and willing to go out with them. In fact, in my opinion, online dating has made most of us single people, women and men, far more disposable in general.

Another path

Good news: single women can choose to take another

path. These days, with the help of social media, women are now normalizing being single and child-free. Some of my favorite thought leaders on this topic are social media creators like Heather Orr @hope_peddler, MJ Gray @texasgardenfairy, and Anna Bash @cuntychanel. Many of my own ways of thinking have been influenced by some of their epic videos on the joys and laments of being single.

Single women now have the luxury of designing our own lives, of creating our own security and fun, and of sharing our lives with those who treat us with respect – and who love us unconditionally.

"But I still want love…"

… and you're not alone. The good news is that women can still enjoy a very full life of love until they meet a loving guy, through friendship, family, and loving themselves. The following chapters will explore specific examples on how to do just that.

4. MONEY AND CAREER

HOW MY ROCK BOTTOM TURNED INTO THE
ROCK UPON WHICH I BUILT MY CAREER

The first step to living a remarkable life as a single woman is to get your financial house in order so you can afford the lifestyle of your choosing. Full disclaimer: this may take some time.

But guess what – most coupled-up women have to get their finances straight, too. At least as a single woman, you will have more control over them. You won't have to worry about a husband spending your savings at the bar or on a sports betting app, or making a well-intentioned but risky investment. Or dealing with a man who keeps you in the dark about how much money is coming in – and limits your access to it.

Some women don't want to face their finances at all and decide to marry for money instead. But as the old saying goes, marry for money and you'll pay for the rest of your life. I'd suggest that anyone considering this path go binge-watch *The Real Housewives* immediately. Some of those women's experiences should be considered cautionary tales for all of us.

Besides, as we already discussed, the majority of men

will expect their wives to work after marriage anyway. So everyone should learn how to work as smart as they can in a way they enjoy. And for single women, they will at least have full control over how they spend the fruits of their labors.

Another cautionary tale: me

Conventional advice for building wealth is to work hard, save your money, and invest it wisely. The problem with this advice is that we live in a time where, for many of us, after we work and pay our bills, there's often nothing left to save, let alone invest. That's why it is imperative to get creative with money – both how you make *and* spend it – especially when you're supporting yourself and not splitting the bill.

I was a cautionary tale myself when I was 25. I was renting an apartment I couldn't afford in order "to be close to my job." In reality, the reason was to be close to downtown nightlife and to a guy I was dating. (I use the term "dating" here loosely; it was, in retrospect, more of a situationship – but that word didn't exist yet.) I was making $43,500 a year at a nonprofit job, which wasn't a lot even 16 years ago. Especially when I had a $600/month student loan payment and a penchant for using my new credit card.

The guy I was in a situationship with, let's call him Dave, was a cute accountant in my friend group who could be charming when he wanted to be. This proved to be often in the early stages of our relationship and then rarely towards the end. He prided himself on being a fan of obscure indie music and nonsensical hipster e-zines *(are e-zines still a thing?)*, and if I met him today, I would find him completely insufferable. Sixteen years ago, though, I was flattered when this typically aloof "cool guy" asked me out after a group outing at the bar.

21

The next two years proved to be a roller coaster. Dave and I had some great times together, going to "shows" *(not "concerts," as he corrected me)*, dinner, and watching weird things on TV. But more often than not, I was left reeling. For example, one time Dave and his roommates hosted a party at their house, and he thought I was flirting with his friend. So he glared at me, went to his room, slammed the door, and refused to come back out for the rest of the night.

I was just trying to be nice to his friend, who was from out-of-town, to make him feel welcome. And I should have laughed at Dave's childish behavior and ended things right then and there. But instead I felt terrible that I made him jealous and thought, "Wow, Dave must really like me." *I* apologized to *him* the next day.

A night like this would take place every two or three months or so.

Then there were the times Dave would disappear for weeks on end for seemingly no reason. He wouldn't answer my texts or emails, but I would hear about how he went out with his roommates or our mutual friends. I would get very hurt and upset. In an effort to get over him, I would go out with other guys, thinking it was over between us. But when Dave would somehow catch wind of that, he would send me an email apologizing for being MIA, referencing a childhood trauma, and saying that he sometimes just "shuts down" and needs some time to himself.

I finally had enough of hearing this excuse and decided to distance myself from Dave as much as I could. But this was difficult since we lived in a small city and had a lot of mutual friends. And I still had feelings for him, even though I knew the relationship wasn't a healthy one. But I couldn't keep explaining away his bad behavior just because he had a traumatic experience.

One night we were both at a party at a mutual friend's house. I brought my new neighbor, a nice girl from Russia named Nadia who was looking to make friends in the area.

Dave had reached out to me a few days earlier and asked if we could hang out one-on-one, and I said I would see him with everyone else at the party later that week. Well, I don't think he liked this answer.

That night, Dave seemed to further feel the distance between us and didn't seem to like that I was no longer a rapt audience – so he started flirting and paying close attention to Nadia, who had no idea that I used to date him. They were beer pong partners throughout the evening, and I saw them leave the party together later that night.

When I returned home an hour later myself, I laid in bed frozen, unable to sleep. Nadia lived literally right next door to me, and Dave was probably with her at that very moment, doing God knows what.

The next afternoon I knocked on Nadia's door, where she excitedly confirmed they hooked up and that she really liked him. I felt sick to my stomach.

Talk about a mind-fuck.

A quarter-life crisis turns into a quarter-life opportunity

After Nadia told me that she and Dave hooked up, I faked a smile, said "that's great," and returned to my apartment, where I curled up on the couch and cried. I wasn't upset with Nadia – she was just a pawn in Dave's game – but I was shaken by Dave's mind games and bitterly disappointed that he was now so clearly not "The One." I guess a part of me was hoping he'd change his ways and we could be together. But my sense of pride finally emerged stronger than my feelings for him. There was no way I could be with him now.

And another fact became clear: I no longer wanted to live in this too-small city or in this apartment I couldn't even afford, which was located right next to Dave's new situationship.

So I turned to my parents.

My parents lived about 20 minutes away in the suburbs and always told me that I should live with them and commute to my office to save money. I always laughed off their suggestions, saying only losers live with their parents after a "certain age."

Well, I officially joined the loser club. Except it turned out to not be the loser club at all. Returning home ended up being one of the best things I ever did for myself, giving me space to heal, rein in my spending habits, and decide what I really wanted to do with my life. I also gradually distanced myself from my old group of local friends, who turned out to be mostly Dave apologists.

Not only was I lucky enough to have the love and support of my parents and family in one of my darkest hours, but I was also able to save all the money I had been throwing away towards rent, utilities, and parking tickets. (After I paid off my thousands of dollars in credit card debt, that is.) My mom made me write her a check in the amount of my old rent and utilities every month, and she put it into an account I could not access. She also seized my credit card.

After two years (yes, two years), I was finally ready to flee the nest again and move two hours away to a much bigger city. I asked for the $8,000 I had saved after paying off my credit card, but my parents said no – not unless I was going to use it to buy a house or make a wise investment. I made a show of pouting, but ultimately knew they were right.

About six months after I moved, I decided I loved my new city and wanted to lay down roots. So I started looking for a house to buy. There was no way I could carry a mortgage on my own – I was still making less than $50,000 at this point, while holding onto student loan debt. And with no boyfriend in sight, I would have to get roommates, although this was admittedly less than ideal.

I was complaining about this to my sister and brother-in-law over lunch one day. My brother-in-law, who is a real estate developer and a Good Guy if there ever was one, suggested that I look into buying a duplex, where I could live in one unit and rent out the other. If done correctly, he said, the renters would be paying most of the mortgage, and I would be able to have my own private space.

I brushed his suggestion off at first, thinking *yeah right, so I would be a landlord?* I wouldn't know the first thing about finding renters, making repairs, or dealing with city regulations.

But the more I looked at houses to buy and experienced issues with roommates, the more attractive buying a duplex seemed. I told my realtor to include duplexes and even triplexes in the search, and we ended up finding a somewhat dated but very cute duplex for sale for around $200,000.

The neighborhood was on the seedy side, but it was just a few blocks away from a much nicer neighborhood and only a mile away from downtown, which was totally walkable. This also meant I wouldn't need a car and could save money by avoiding a car payment, gas, and insurance – as well as parking tickets.

The mortgage would be about $1400 a month. The renters who were living in the other unit – who would go on to stay there for the next five years – paid about $1000 a month. That meant I would only be spending $400 of my own money on the mortgage each month – which was far less than what I spent in rent on my last apartment.

I bought the duplex. It was the best investment I ever made.

Minimize your expenses

Buying a duplex or other type of multi-family home (or even a single-family home with roommates) may not be for everyone. There have definitely been stressful moments over the years, like when I needed to find new renters for the first time or make home repairs.

But it turns out that finding new tenants wasn't that big of a deal. That's what websites like Zillow and Apartments.com are for. And it turns out that there are plenty of great handymen and contractors on other apps that can help with maintenance. Yes, repairs come with a cost, but I rarely needed to make them. And since I was only paying $400 out of my own pocket for the mortgage, I was able to afford it.

My only regret is that my realtor failed to inform me that the property was not zoned correctly. So if you ever want to buy a duplex or other property, be sure to ask your realtor to do their due diligence. Ask if the property has the correct zoning and if there are any outstanding violations on the property. I had to learn this the hard way – but fortunately I was able to work it out in the end.

Buying a duplex or home to share with roommates is a great way to minimize what is typically our largest expense – rent or a mortgage. And to get ahead as a single person, we must be creative in minimizing our expenses as much as we can and avoid making emotional decisions that are not in our financial best interests – no matter how cute the guy is that you're "dating" or what your friends are doing.

For example, when I was 25, it seemed like all my friends were either living on their own in cool cities or were buying traditional single-family homes with their romantic partners. Wanting to keep up, I rented an apartment I couldn't afford and dug myself further into a financial hole, which had already begun with my student loans.

I didn't know anyone living with their parents past the age of 22 or 23 (right when they returned home from college), and I certainly didn't know anyone who had bought a multi-family home. I didn't even know what a multi-family home *was*.

Well, it turns out everyone's circumstances can change. I now know people well into their 30s and 40s who have had to move in with their parents or other family at some point or another. Shit happens to all of us, and it comes in many forms: job loss, serious illness, divorce, or psychological abuse from a dirtbag you're seeing. And those of us fortunate to have family to support us in these hard times should absolutely take advantage of it – and of course return the favor to them, should that day ever come.

Maybe you won't have the option of getting ahead by living at home with your parents or other family. If you know that this will be the case and are still in your teens, you could avoid going into debt at the start of adulthood by refusing to get student loans. Apply for scholarships and grants and consider attending community college or online universities instead. Or skip college altogether, especially if you don't know what you want to do yet.

One of my closest girlfriends was wise enough to do this. She went to community college and worked as a waitress while the rest of our friend group went to state universities and private schools. Twenty years later, she is now COO of a

27

nationally renowned accounting firm with more than 200 employees. She makes more money than the rest of us – *and* has zero student loan debt. (I'm *still* paying my master's degree off.) Talk about minimizing your expenses and maximizing your income!

What if you're older and already have student loans or other high expenses? Rethink and re-examine *all* of your other expenditures that may have gone up or may not really be necessary in the first place. For example, a lot of people have cars, but do *you* really need one? *Be ruthless.*

It's amazing how much bills can creep up over time when contracts expire and you're not paying attention (especially when auto-pay is involved). For example, when my contract for my home security system expired, I started paying 50 percent more on the monthly bill without realizing it, which came out to about $300 more a year. Even though I'm making a lot more money now than I was when the security system was installed, and can technically afford the increase, it is simply not smart to pay so much more for the same service when I don't have to. Because when bills creep up like that, it effectively reduces your income, as well as any gains you worked so hard to make.

So a couple times a year, usually when my business has slower months than usual (more on that in a bit), I go through my bank statements and personal budget spreadsheet line-by-line. (If you don't already have a document like this, make one immediately that lists every single expense you have.) Where possible, I research cheaper options for all of my expenses. Armed with these options, I call my current service providers whose contracts have expired and, very nicely, state that I plan to transfer to another provider unless they can beat, or at least meet, their competition's rates. They almost always humor me and meet or beat the rate.

With my recent call to my security system provider, however, I was so incensed by the huge rate increase I had been unknowingly paying for more than a year, that I didn't even bother researching their competition's rates. Instead I called and said if they didn't revert back to my original rate, I would cancel the service that day. They instantly acquiesced and gave me the original rate I signed up for five years ago. This rate was not available on any promotion; they tailored it for me. (Companies ultimately make their own rules and can usually make rates whatever they want.)

Here are some questions to ask yourself when making your personal budget:

- Again, do you really need that car? Can you walk, use public transit, rideshare, and use grocery delivery services instead? Or get a bike?
- Can you refinance your student loans? I was eventually able to refinance mine at a lower interest rate and over a longer period of time, which reduced the monthly payment from $600 to $350.
- Do you really need cable or all those streaming services?
- Can you find a cheaper internet or cell phone provider? For example, I just switched cell phone plans which reduced my monthly phone bill from $101 to $30, saving me more than $70 each month. And I still get unlimited talk, text, *and* data. There is virtually no difference in quality from my last cell phone provider. I also just changed my internet provider, saving me $36 a month.
- Can you and your friends or family create a cellphone family plan? That way you divide the total bill two,

three, or more ways.

- Are you actually using that expensive gym or Pilates membership? Can you do pay-what-you-can classes or watch a video online instead? (If you *are* using the membership, great; keep it.)
- Can you cut back on how often you go out to eat or drink? Consider creating a supper club with your friends where you take turns cooking for each other or bring dishes to each other's homes. This is often a lot more intimate and fun, anyway.
- If you live in a city, can you limit grocery delivery services to only when you need heavy items or to stock up on something, and walk to the grocery store to buy other items as you need them? It's great exercise, and you not only save on fees and tip, but also prices of goods, which tend to be lower in-store.
- Do you really need to live in an expensive city like New York or Los Angeles, especially in the age of remote work? In addition to skyrocketing housing costs, NYC and LA in particular have higher taxes than a lot of other places, which can essentially serve as a pay cut – especially as you start earning more money. Do some online research into the tax structure of the cities you're considering moving to before taking the plunge. I personally like to play around on the SmartAsset.com income tax calculator – they have one for every state. (Always consult a certified CPA accountant on your taxes, however.)

Reconsidering whether you really need to live in an expensive city can especially save you money. When I first began living at home with my parents, I was determined to move out as soon as possible and find a job in New York City. I don't know if I thought I would be the next Carrie Bradshaw or what, but a part of me seemed to think that making it in New York would prove my worth to Dave and anyone else whom I perceived to have wronged me.

Well, the only company in New York to tentatively offer me a job didn't want to pay me much more than what I was already making in a far cheaper, less cosmopolitan city. I was struggling enough as it was to survive on $43,500, but I tried looking for a NYC apartment on that budget anyway. However, the only places I could afford were hellholes where I would have to share a bedroom and not have anything left over in my budget to spend. As much as I wanted to take the job, I knew the numbers just didn't make sense.

Turns out these kinds of numbers don't work for a lot of people. According to *New York Magazine*,[16] there are a lot more fully grown adults living in New York getting financial help from their families than you might think. But getting that much help from my parents wasn't an option for me – and it's not an option for most.

I was disappointed the New York job didn't work out, but in the long run, I am so happy. I moved to an even better city (in my opinion) instead, one of the ten largest in the country, and I paid $400 a month for a space that would have cost about $4,000 in New York.

And you can do the same. Save New York (or California) for when you become more established – if you even still want to live there at that point.

---

[16] Paula Aceves et al., "People with Parents with Money," *New York Magazine*, February 2025, last accessed June 13, 2025, https://nymag.com/intelligencer/article/parents-money-family-wealth-stories.html.

Maximize your income

Now let's rethink how you *make* your money. There are different schools of thought on this. Some "experts" advise people against side hustles so they can give their full-time job everything they've got. However, I would only advise going this route if you're already making a six-figure salary – and/or six-figure bonuses. Like a finance or tech job where they often make more than $200,000 a year and thousands of dollars more in commissions, bonuses, and stock options. Then yes, I agree – give that job all you've got! But if you are only making $70,000 a year (or as was my case for years, around $50,000), providing hours of overtime without extra compensation will likely never get you ahead.

I recommend giving your employer all you've got from nine to five – or nine to six at the most – and then getting the hell out to make more money. Or scrapping the full-time job for more unconventional ways to make money instead.

Going back to when I bought my duplex – I was saving a ton of money by renting out the other unit in my property, refinancing my student loans, and giving up a car. In fact, the combination of doing all these things was the equivalent of giving myself a $15,000 salary increase. So I was significantly better off than I was before. But two years in, I was still only making a little more than $50,000 a year at my communications nonprofit job. I was applying for other positions advertised at $60-70k a year, but I soon realized that $60-70k, after taxes, was not going to dramatically change my lifestyle. I wanted to be making $100k or more, but I couldn't see how that could happen in my field, at least at my level of experience.

That is, until an old boss of mine, Sue, approached me

with a consulting offer. Many people don't really understand what consulting is – maybe because it has a slightly different definition for everyone who does it. For me, consulting is essentially independent part-time work for clients in a specialized niche. While I still have to meet client deadlines, I'm usually able to make my own schedule to meet those deadlines, and I usually work off-site, whether from home, while traveling, in my own office, etc. I can charge hourly or on a monthly retainer (usually retainer), which often means I make more money than people with full-time jobs in the same industry.

Sue offered me a communications consulting gig at her nonprofit for a monthly retainer of about $3,000, or $36,000 a year. However, I knew that my current employer would never let me take on that contract while also working full-time for them – and because our specific sector was a small one, the organization would definitely find out what I was up to. I asked Sue if she could possibly pay me more so I could leave my full-time job, and she said no – but reminded me that I could of course get as many other clients as I wanted, as long as I continued to do a good job for her organization.

A lightbulb went off over my head. What if I got at least two more clients that each paid at least $36,000? I'd be making more than $100,000 a year! And even if I got just *one* more client at $36,000, it would bring me to $72,000, a big jump from the $54,000 I was making at my current job.

However, I would have to take a step backward before I could move forward (which is often the case in business). In other words, I would have to take a pay cut and survive on $36,000 while I looked for more clients. It helped that my renters were covering the majority of my mortgage, and that I already gave up my car and refinanced my student loans – making me grateful to my former self for making those decisions. If I further cut my expenses – to the bone (no cable, no going out to dinner, etc.) – I could make this work.

I also realized that, as a single child-free woman, I had the privilege of taking a risk like this. I didn't have small children depending on me, so if consulting didn't work out, it's not like I had extra mouths to feed. If I did get desperate for money, I could try to defer student loan or mortgage payments while I searched for more clients. That wouldn't be ideal since interest would continue to accrue, but it could work if I was in a tight spot.

So I took a leap of faith, quit my full-time job, and never looked back.

Consulting life

I now love being a consultant and all the freedom and extra income it provides. Consulting is a win-win for everyone – the client doesn't have to pay the consultant a full-time salary with benefits, and the consultant gets to make more money than they would at a full-time job, if done properly. Isn't this kind of win-win the very definition of good business?

No two years are the same, though. While you might be killing it one year, the next year you might lose a client – or three, as I did during the pandemic. And consulting requires doing your best, all the time, to keep your clients impressed, as well as good money management. You want to build enough money in savings to dip into in case you lose a client, which sometimes happens no matter how much they love you. Sometimes their budgets will get slashed or they'll need to hire someone full-time, and that has nothing to do with you.

It's also not that easy to find new clients. It took me a

year to find my second client (I explain how in Chapter 7 – I almost gave up), but then I more quickly found a third, and then a fourth, thanks to referrals from my second client. (Another reason you always want to do your best – you never know who is watching and might refer you.) And my bigger and for-profit clients have paid me much more than my first non-profit one did – about $5-6,000 a month *each*.

I have had some clients for about five years now, but like I said, you never know when one will go away once a six-month or one-year-long contract ends. So if you take the consulting route, save, save, save your money and be sure to put enough aside for taxes, health insurance, and other expenses. But with all that said, I have successfully been making six figures a year on a regular basis, apart from my first year and during the pandemic era. I hope to eventually be able to hire someone to help me and start building a full communications agency.

Other paths

Consulting isn't the only avenue to building financial freedom, however. Maybe you want to start slowly and keep your full-time job while having a part-time side hustle. Technology is making it much easier to do that at scale, removing old industry gatekeepers and democratizing the business landscape. Here are just a few side hustle ideas and resources that could eventually help you turn your pet interest into a full-fledged business:

- Sell a product online[17] or directly to consumers via social media ads. If applicable, look into

---

[17] "How to Sell on Amazon: a guide for beginners." Amazon, last accessed on June 13, 2025, https://sell.amazon.com/sell.

manufacturers who specialize in making a unit of your product only after a customer places an order for it, known as "Build to Order" or "Make to Order." This can both avoid waste and the need to make an expensive upfront investment in inventory.

- Create videos online or on social media on whatever topics interest you. If you get enough followers and views, you can get paid through ads, sponsorships, and any product sales.
- Create a blog, newsletter, or social media account on a niche topic and include affiliate links, ads, and brand partnerships.
- Host a website or podcast on a niche topic and get advertisers. It can be super easy to make your own website these days (Squarespace is my preferred platform), and resources are available on how to maximize site traffic, which in turn can equal more money from advertisers. As for podcasts, many successful podcasts offer 1-2 free episodes every week on Spotify and Apple Podcasts and then an extra one each week behind a paywall on apps like Patreon. If you can get just 1,000 Patreon subscribers at $5/month, that's $5,000.
- Sell tickets for pop-up dinners, concerts, or art shows at your home or another cool location you have access to, advertised on social media. Ask local or related brands for sponsorships or partnerships and include them in your marketing and event experience. (Make sure to check for any prohibitive local laws and ordinances.)
- Walk dogs or offer pet-sitting services and advertise on community Facebook groups and other platforms. Build up your social media presence and then build

partnerships or sponsorships with pet brands.

- If you're a teacher, offer tutoring services and create a social media presence around it, without violating your students' privacy. Eventually approach educational businesses for paid sponsorships or partnerships.
- Write and self-publish a book (on Amazon for example),[18] which can often make the author far more money than going with a traditional book publisher.

These are just a few ideas, and since I'm a communications professional, I realize they are heavily skewed towards leveraging social media and other forms of marketing. I encourage you to pursue what feels most natural to you, or what you have felt envious of other people doing. I for one would never want to make videos online or host a podcast; public speaking has never been my thing. But you might love it, find it easy, and love the money it can generate.

Many books and resources on how to do most of these things are just an online search away. Be sure to check with an accountant on the best way to pay taxes on your earnings. You may want to start an LLC or S Corporation, which can be easy to do. Also see if you can get free advice from your local U.S. Small Business Administration on common pitfalls and legal issues in the industry you're trying to get into.

Service professions are often harder to convert to businesses or side hustles, as you may have had to sign a non-compete agreement with your full-time employer. But maybe

---

[18] Matt Rudnitsky, *You Are An Author: So Write Your Book Already* (Platypus Publications, 2016).

you can get out of, or wait out, the non-compete stipulations. If you can, ask to meet with people who are running a successful business similar to the one you envision and ask them for tips on getting started. They'll likely be flattered you asked and may even send you referrals, which are prospective clients they had to turn away due to a conflict of interest or because their business was too busy. (This has happened to me many times in the past.)

Also, consider asking them how much they charge their clients, if you feel comfortable enough with them. If that seems too brazen, maybe consider saying something like, "I'm having trouble figuring out how much to charge my clients," and see if they volunteer any valuable information. If you're just getting started, consider charging just half to two-thirds of what they charge and include your rate in proposals to prospective clients. That could be enough to convince a prospect to take a chance with someone less established like you instead of a bigger consulting firm.

We all make mistakes along the way, so don't beat yourself up when you ultimately do, too. It's part of the process and worth your freedom and financial security in the end.

Can I just ask for more money at my full-time job?

You might be wondering how to just convince your existing employer to pay you more or how to find a higher paying full-time job. I personally was only ever able to secure small raises at a time (think less than $5,000), which wasn't significant enough for the lifestyle I wanted, but you can certainly try. Honestly, I think pursuing a side hustle or new business is more worth your time in the long run. I have friends who have searched for *years* for significantly higher-paying full-time jobs to no avail. In fact as I write this, they are still looking. And these are smart women with MBAs and other advanced degrees. (This is also why I don't recommend spending tens to hundreds of thousands of dollars on college or grad school.)

It is, in my opinion, much more empowering to start your own business where the sky is the limit than to beg someone else for crumbs. With self-discipline and commitment, my business has blossomed into something far more lucrative than that $10-20,000 salary bump I was once looking for. Try not to waste your time.

Saving and Investing

Years after buying the duplex and finally succeeding at consulting, I hit the sweet spot of both dramatically minimizing my expenses and maximizing my income. I finally had significant money left over each month! So what was next? I saved and invested it all, right?

Wrong. I bought a designer bag from Maison Margiela and went on a trip to Tulum, Mexico (among other things).

Oh, how I wish I had that money just months later when a big client dropped me – and then when another one did. I felt like the universe – or God – was teaching me a lesson.

I was still doing better financially than when I first started consulting, but I was still like, *Come on. Can't I have any fun at all?*

I would eventually learn that yes, I could have fun, but I also needed to put aside enough money every month to build an emergency fund that would cover at least three, if not six, months of expenses. And some budding investments, like stocks or bonds.

The good news is that I already had one major

investment in place – my home and rental unit. Multi-family properties like mine are wonderful investments because, as Scott Galloway says in *The Algebra of Wealth*,[19] mortgage payments are like "forced savings." Sure, a lot of the mortgage payment is interest and property tax, but a hefty portion is actually money you will get back someday when you sell the property. For example, I bought my property for $203,000 about 12 years ago, and I have been paying it down a little bit every month since. Once the mortgage is completely paid off and I sell the house, I should get all of that $203,000 back, plus whatever the increased value of the property is. Online estimates say that today the property is worth approximately $450,000. Can you imagine what it could be worth in 18 years? (I go into more detail on how I bought and renovated the house in Chapter 8.)

Plus, I might not even want to sell it at that time. I hope to buy another property for myself well before that – maybe another duplex – and rent out both units of the property I'm in now, to create a stream of passive income. But it will ultimately depend on how much property values fluctuate and what the rental market is like.

In the meantime, I am enjoying my money while also building – and re-building – that fucking emergency fund, and learning about the stock market and mutual funds. In addition to reading books like *The Algebra of Wealth* and *Rich Dad, Poor Dad*[20] by Robert T. Kiyosaki, I have a couple of free apps on my phone that let me play-invest in the stock market – I suggest you check some of those out, as well.

I have also tried my hand at other businesses and

---

[19] Scott Galloway, *The Algebra of Wealth: A Simple Formula for Financial Security* (Portfolio, 2024).

[20] Robert Kiyosaki, *Rich Dad, Poor Dad: What the Rich Teach Their Kids About Money That the Poor and Middle Class Do Not!* (Plata Publishing, 2022).

investments over the past several years, in addition to consulting and real estate. These included a travel business and buying an abandoned coal mine (don't ask). These efforts were ultimately not successful, but at least I learned a lot about partnering with other people and liability issues in the process. They were also a good exercise in trying to think outside the box to create a solid consumer product. So I'm glad I tried, and I'm going to continue to try.

In particular, I always keep an eye out for some kind of passive investment that could reap a ton of money down the road. For example, a plot of land for sale in a given location might become very valuable one day. If the land is cheap, and if I have enough money for a down payment and can afford the monthly loan payment, I might go for it. But it also comes back to how much I have saved in that emergency fund.

A leap of faith

The hardest part about starting a new business is often just having the balls to do it. A lot of people are too scared to take a leap of faith like that – maybe because they don't have faith in themselves or in a higher power to begin with. I personally attribute my own faith in a higher power to making these leaps easier for me.

Look, I know it doesn't sound cool or intellectual to talk about God or spirituality, and I hope this isn't the point where I lose you as my audience. But it would be misleading if I claimed my success was achieved all on my own. Whatever you may call it – God, Allah, the universe, manifestation – I don't recommend going through life, or starting a business, without it.

I grew up Catholic but stopped going to church as soon as I went to college. While at college, I never prayed, never thought about God or a higher power at all. I vaguely believed in God but didn't think it was cool or necessary to talk about it. And let's be honest, the Catholic Church has made some horrific mistakes over the years, to put it mildly. Who were *they* to tell me how to live?

It took me hitting rock bottom when I was 26 and moving back in with my parents to get me to reflect on the role God did or didn't play in my predicament. My parents made me start going to church with them again (a live-at-home tax). I also read *The Secret*[21] by Rhonda Byrne for the first time, which is about manifestation and the law of attraction.

I had nothing else going on at the time and decided to give manifestation a try. I began by visualizing myself earning $10,000 more than I was at the time. *(Why was I so fixated on this number?)* I made a vision board, wrote in my journal about it, and thought about it before I went to sleep. I pretended I already received it, as the book suggests, and tried to feel the joy it would bring me.

Well, a few months later, I won $10,000 worth of lip gloss from a large, big-box retailer.

Really. The store even named a lip gloss after me, a bright peachy pink. The situation was both hilarious and highly disappointing.

I ended up selling most of the lip gloss on eBay and made a measly $1,000, which was nowhere close to the $1,300 or so I had to pay in taxes on the lip gloss. But I did take the prize as a sign that the universe was listening.

My Catholic parents, bemused but happy I was finally doing *something* spiritual, encouraged me to try praying the regular way instead. Every day, not just at church on Sundays. So I did, but I still grew increasingly frustrated.

---

[21] Rhonda Byrne, *The Secret* (Fang Zhi/Tsai Fong Books, 2007).

My mother reminded me that when we ask God for something, the answer is always one of three things: 1) "Yes." 2) "Not yet." or 3) "I have something better in mind."

Slowly but surely, things got a lot better in my life. I eventually received some small pay raises – adding up to about $10,000 – moved to a city I loved, and found new ways to save money to further maximize my income. And finally, God's ultimate answer to my prayers transitioned to number three – that he had something far better in mind. Like earning more than six figures a year.

Want me to let you in on another little Catholic secret? During the pandemic, I was on unemployment for months while desperately searching for new clients. I was also trying to get one of those extra small business grants from the federal government. The guidelines suggested I was eligible for one up to $10,000, so I applied and tried to call the administrative office every couple of weeks to follow up. However, I always had trouble getting through – probably because every business in the country wanted that money.

Finally, after months of waiting, I heard reports about how the grant fund was dwindling and was about to close. Anguished, I decided to finally follow a piece of my father's advice I had long ignored: pray the Rosary. The Rosary is a collection of Catholic prayers directed more towards Mary (Jesus' mother) than to Jesus or to God. In the Rosary, you say almost 70 prayers in one sitting – six Our Fathers, 53 Hail Marys, six Glory Bes, and a few other longer prayers. I hadn't said one since my Polish grandmother was alive, when she made us pray the Rosary together whenever we took a long car ride.

I found a video online that could guide me in saying it, as I was rusty. It didn't take me as long as I thought, maybe 15 minutes. And guess what?

$10,000 miraculously appeared in my checking account just a few days later. And that was in cash, not lip gloss.

I guess that's what happens when you get a woman involved.

Listen, I can't pretend to have any definitive answers when it comes to spirituality. But I also can't in good conscience tell you to make major moves like starting a business or buying a duplex without having a spiritual safety net.

If you want to read up more on this on your own, some books I highly recommend include *The Universe has Your Back: Transform Fear to Faith*[22] by Gabrielle Bernstein; *Conversations with God: An Uncommon Dialogue*[23] by Neale Donalde Walsch; and *Rich Dad, Poor Dad: What the Rich Teach Their Kids About Money That the Poor and Middle Class Do Not!*[24] by Robert Kiyosaki. There is always, of course, the Bible, but it can be incredibly difficult to read without context and proper interpretation. I also personally suspect that some parts of the Bible have been tampered with over the years to serve various political and ideological agendas, although its underlying message of love and faith still rings true.

You also have to have faith in *yourself* and learn not to pay attention to haters or even well-meaning but overly cautious loved ones. I cannot tell you how many people told

---

[22] Gabrielle Bernstein, *The Universe has Your Back: Transform Fear to Faith* (Hay House, 2025).

[23] Neale Donalde Walsch, *Conversations with God: An Uncommon Dialogue* (G.P. Putnam's Sons, 1996).

[24] Robert Kiyosaki, *What the Rich Teach Their Kids About Money That the Poor and Middle Class Do Not!* (Plata Publishing, 2022).

me I shouldn't buy the duplex or start consulting – even my own parents, who were worried that I didn't know what I was getting myself into. They were right about that, but they were wrong that I wouldn't be able to handle it. And for that, I thank God.

5. HEALTH AND BODY
SKINNY AND BROKE VS. CHUBBY WITH MONEY

I hope you weren't hoping to find a workout regimen or strict diet here – because as a single woman, you have the freedom to eat whatever the hell you want. More retro books like *Sex and the Single Girl* stressed the importance of maintaining your figure to attract men, encouraging the eating of carrot sticks for lunch and the "least glopped up item" on the menu when dining out. You will find none of that kind of advice here.

Now with that said, since many of us are supporting ourselves, yes, we have to take care as much as we can to avoid illness and to keep ourselves sharp for work. Modern-day wisdom tells us that a reasonably balanced diet and exercise that you enjoy can play a major role in both physical and mental health.

However, there are certain foods that I used to eat every day since childhood that, as I discovered in my late 20s, had been holding me back my entire life. I will talk a little bit more about that in this section to help you decide if you would like to do some experimenting on your own to learn if any of your go-to foods have, unbeknownst to you, been affecting your health and well-being.

With that said, though, depriving yourself just to look a certain way – especially for someone else's benefit – is as retro as it gets.

A bodily revolt

I haven't always had this attitude towards my body. And now, at age 41, it kills me that I wasted years in my 20s and 30s thinking I was fat and doing juice cleanses or 24-hour "fasts" to lose three pounds or to be able fit into a size four.

News alert: no one ever needs to know what size you're wearing or how much you weigh (besides medical professionals). A lot of women especially tend to get caught up in the size of their clothing, when every brand is different and the number is ultimately meaningless. I personally have become so much more comfortable, and look so much better, accepting the sizes that are actually meant for my body.

The truth is that most people are too busy obsessing about their own bodies to care about yours. Really. If anything, I have found that putting on a few pounds over the past few years has made me better liked by other women. Is that messed up? Maybe, if it's because it makes them feel superior or like I'm less of a threat. But maybe it has nothing to do with my appearance and it's because I now subconsciously have a more accepting and likable attitude towards myself and therefore others. I suspect it's the latter.

Don't get me wrong, I still like to look my best. But I've stopped overestimating how much my weight has to do with this. For me, great skincare, volumizing hair products, high-quality makeup, and flattering, comfortable, yet stylish clothes make me feel and look great. Add a good non-toxic perfume and fresh mani-pedi, and I feel even better.

But I've only had this perspective for a few years.

When I was 38, my body seemed to be revolting against me. I used to be able to stay within a certain range on the scale by eating around 2,000 calories a day, as long as I did hot yoga a few days a week. But suddenly, eating the same way I had for years made my jeans too tight. I also found that drinking alcohol made my face puffy the next day, and it also caused me to sleep terribly, making me toss and turn and sweat all night long.

I decided it was time for a change, a major one. I have done various cleanses about once or twice a year since I was 27 – juice cleanses, raw food cleanses, even a Master cleanse (which I would never do again and would never, ever recommend to anyone else). But in order to lose the 15 pounds I had seemingly put on overnight, I wanted to do more of a lifestyle change that I could easily adjust to once I hit my goal weight. I decided on an "elimination diet" where you eat real food but eliminate foods that a lot of people are sensitive to without even realizing it – wheat/gluten, dairy, eggs, soy, corn, caffeine, and alcohol – and try to eat as organic and unprocessed as possible.

The diet lasts for three weeks and is followed by a phase where you re-introduce the eliminated foods one at a time each day to see how your body responds to them. If there is no negative bodily reaction to the food item, then it's not considered an "allergen" for you and you could return to eating it. More details can be found in the book *Clean: The Revolutionary Program to Restore the Body's Natural Ability to Heal Itself* by Dr. Alejandro Junger.[25]

I had done this diet many times before and already knew what my triggers were, but I had heard that we can

---

[25] Dr. Alejandro Junger, *Clean: The Revolutionary Program to Restore the Body's Natural Ability to Heal Itself* (Harper One, 2010).

become allergic to new things as we get older. I also wanted to go through the whole process again and do it as a reset -- because I had stopped applying everything I had learned when I began dating a Good Guy named Eric.

Eric and I had been friends first, and then one night after a happy hour, he asked if he could kiss me. I said yes, and soon we found ourselves hanging out several nights a week – almost always going out for dinner after work or cooking together at one of our homes. We both loved food, trying new restaurants, and trying to recreate dishes we saw online. We also enjoyed good wine with our meals.

However, I soon realized that five months of this lifestyle, combined with my body's increased intolerance of certain foods, was contributing to my 15-pound weight gain. Something had to change. So I embarked on the elimination diet.

Well, this meant I had to tell Eric what I was doing. And he, of course, looked at me like I was crazy. "First of all, you don't need to lose weight," he said. "And secondly, if you do want to lose weight, this isn't the way to do it."

It was easy for him to say. Eric was a big guy – about 6'2" and somewhat burly, but not overweight at all. He could eat probably twice what I was eating and still not be considered overweight.

"Is this why you've only been ordering fish and vegetables lately?" Eric demanded. "And refuse to try the brownies I made?"

"Yes," I admitted. "But it's not forever, just until I get to my goal weight."

"What then?" Eric asked. "You're just going to put the weight back on. You have to find a more sustainable way."

He was a thousand percent correct, but I didn't want to be mansplained to about *my* body by a guy who could eat whatever he wanted. I repeated to him that it would be over in three weeks.

"But I don't get it. So you're never going to have bread again? Or a drink? What the fuck. Don't you want to enjoy your life?"

I seriously regretted being honest with him about what I was doing. I should have pretended that I just wasn't that hungry anymore, like so many other women do. Or just take one bite of whatever he wanted me to try and then shut up. But now Eric was watching me like a hawk.

After a few days of this sort of back-and-forth, I decided Eric was right. This diet was not sustainable or enjoyable. If the guy I was dating thought I looked good enough, that's all that mattered, right? (So wrong.)

So I stopped doing the elimination diet and returned to drinking and eating whatever I wanted with Eric. I re-gained the few pounds I had lost and decided to practice self-love and body acceptance.

Well, a few weeks later, Eric took me to his golf club for a summer barbeque. I had to buy a new dress that accommodated my new body, and I chose one that was loose and which hid my arms and the boldest of my new curves – namely my hips and butt. When he picked me up, Eric scanned me up and down and visibly rolled his eyes.

When we arrived at the club, Eric began introducing me to his friends and their significant others. We began drinking, heavily, as it was an open bar, with champagne and liquor flowing. I began noticing how Eric's eyes were drawn to the many scantily clad younger women at the party and how attentive he was when any of them came over to say hello. One woman in particular had her breasts spilling out of her dress when she came over and almost pushed me aside to throw her arms around him. They laughed about a round of golf they played the week before.

He didn't bother introducing me. I scowled and went to the buffet, where I started putting together my second plate of food. I was probably four drinks in at this point and was throwing even more caution to the wind as far as my diet was concerned. *Fuck it! And fuck Eric.*

He was still talking to her when I exited the buffet line, and even sent me a look of disgust while I was holding my plate. I wandered over to a couple of women I met earlier that evening, who were married to or dating some of Eric's friends. "Do you guys know that girl?" I asked them, nodding over to Eric.

"Yeah, she's so annoying," said one of the women, rolling her eyes at them. "Always flirting with everyone's husbands. Don't worry, you're so much cuter than she is."

"I'm not worried. I'm done," I said with my mouth full, enjoying the cheese I had been trying to avoid. The women looked alarmed.

I said it was nice to meet them and started walking over to the parking lot while finishing my plate. I called a rideshare and left.

A miscommunication?

"Where are you?"

"Wtf? Did you leave?"

These were the texts waiting for me when I got back to my place and finally looked at my phone. I could feel it vibrating in my pocket during the ride home but was too busy seething with rage to look at it.

I felt like I had been tricked. Tricked into not taking care of myself, into thinking that Eric liked or even preferred how I looked now, compared to how I used to look – or to how other thinner, younger women look.

I called him.

"Hi, yes, I left," I said. "I'm home now."

"Why the fuck did you leave?"

"I'm surprised you even noticed."

"What the fuck, Greta. Is this about that girl I was talking to?"

"Her and all the other girls you were staring at all night."

"Oh my god, you are crazy. Are you serious right now?"

"Don't call me crazy, asshole!" I almost started to cry. I began to feel a pit in my stomach. Had I really misjudged the situation? No. He had been checking out other girls all night, I was certain of it, and he didn't even bother introducing me to the last one. "And I saw the look you gave me before I left. Didn't like that I got seconds, huh?"

"What the *hell* are you talking about? I was trying to relay that I didn't want to talk to that girl anymore; I wanted you to come rescue me."

"Oh, yeah, right. You're a grown man, you can rescue yourself. It's called excusing yourself from the conversation and being a gentleman to the woman you brought as your date." I hung up.

Then I passed out.

When I woke up the next day, I had that excruciating, hungover feeling of regret, of having done or said too much. I immediately checked my phone. There was one text from Eric, sent about an hour before I woke up. "We have to talk."

Oh boy. I closed my eyes and rested my pounding head. Well, this was it. The end with Eric. I was still pissed at his behavior, but, with the drunken haze lifting, I was already beginning to wonder if my reaction had more to do with me – and my own insecurities.

I texted Eric back and we arranged to get coffee later that day. I tried to schedule it for the next day when I felt – and looked – better, but he insisted we talk as soon as possible.

I arrived at the coffee shop on time, despite a tickle in my throat and suspicion that a cold was looming. *Another one?* I wondered. *I just got over one a few weeks ago.* Eric was about 15 minutes late. This was typical of him, and also the main cause of our arguments up to this point. I couldn't believe he couldn't even be on time at this moment, when we were so clearly experiencing a crisis.

He entered the shop and gave me a look. He pulled out his chair and sat down. "Want to tell me what that was all about last night?"

I decided I was going to tell him exactly how I felt. "It was about how you can't stop checking out other girls, and even flirting with them in front of me," I blurted. "If you want to date other people, you're welcome to. Just let me know; I'd like to be on the same page."

"Jesus Christ, I don't want to date other people! I'm sorry if you thought I was checking them out. It's just a guy thing, we can't help ourselves, especially when they're dressed like that. But I don't like those girls."

"You and that girl at the end were totally ignoring me. It was like I wasn't even there."

"I was just trying to get us away from her as soon as possible, and then you ditched me. She's not even attractive. I don't know what you're talking about."

"I could tell you didn't like how I looked. You gave me a weird look when you picked me up."

"I thought that dress was an odd choice, to be honest. It's like you were trying to hide in that thing. I like to see a little skin." He wiggled his eyebrows at me.

"Well, I can't wear stuff like that anymore because I have to eat crap with you all the time!"

"Whoa," Eric said, staring at me. "I don't even think this about me anymore."

He was right of course – at least partially. I was losing control over my body, and it felt like I was being forced to choose between the body of my youth and "enjoying my life" … whatever that means.

But I felt that Eric was also wrong to be telling me what I should or should not be putting into my body. He meant well, yes. I think he wanted me to feel like he supported me no matter what I looked like. But if I wanted to make some positive changes for my well-being, shouldn't he support me then as well?

What I really wanted Eric to do – what I *needed* for him to do – was to shut up about how I was eating and let me figure things out for myself. It quite frankly wasn't any of his business. But he had this weird, entitled attitude that, since he didn't care about my weight, I shouldn't care. Like his opinion was the only one that mattered.

It's my *fucking body, dude*, I thought. And it was my life, not his.

Eric and I didn't last long after this. Food choices became a lightning rod that derailed too many conversations. I could not get him to understand that as long as he was dating me, he wanted two conflicting things: a woman who would eat whatever he wanted her to eat and a woman with a hot, lithe body. In other words, he wanted *me* to proverbially have *his* cake and eat it, too.

Enough is enough

It has been my experience that, just as there is a fine line between eating healthy and an eating disorder, there can also be a fine line between body positivity and overindulgence.

For the next couple of years, I alternated between eating whatever I wanted and embracing my body as it was to suddenly no longer feeling comfortable in my skin and experiencing lower energy levels, joint pain, and mild depression. I would go on sprees where I would have several glasses of wine in one sitting and eat anything on the menu, and then go on such strict diets that dining out or even just in the watchful company of others was nearly impossible.

Then one day, around the age of 40, I decided enough was enough. Weight gain is, for many women, an inevitable part of getting older – unless you resort to a weight loss drug or plastic surgery, neither of which I have any desire to try (*yet*, at least). I decided I was *done* obsessing about my weight – for real this time.

I threw out my scale and gave away all the clothes I had been trying to fit back into. (Now I at least had a good excuse to go shopping.) I also put away the "inspiration photo" of myself from my twenties that I had put on my refrigerator. No one should ever try to compete with how they looked in their twenties. That should be considered cruel and unusual punishment.

I decided, going forward, I would consume mostly only what tasted good *and* made my body feel good. If I went overboard one day, I could try to rein it in the next, but absolutely no "fasting," aka starving myself, was allowed. I would feed myself how I would like my loved ones to eat – with nourishing but delicious food.

I also made some more ground rules for myself,

knowing that rules would, paradoxically enough, give me mental freedom from food. The goal for these rules is to help me *feel* my best, not look my skinniest, and to give me the energy and clarity I need to support myself and truly enjoy my life.

I encourage you to come up with a list of rules that work specifically for you that help you feel good and maintain your optimal health and well-being. This may take some experimentation.

For example, I have done enough elimination diets over the years to know that I have real sensitivities to gluten and dairy, and that they create chaos in my system. Chaos that manifests in a variety of ways, including acne, joint pain, brain fog, constipation, and colds. In fact, I suspect that gluten and dairy are behind the many colds I always had growing up. From the time when I was a child to age 27, I would have on average six colds a year. Every change of season, like clockwork, I would get a terrible cold and would be exhausted. And then an extra two or three colds would be sprinkled throughout the year for good measure.

When I did my first elimination diet when I was 27 and continued to try to avoid or minimize gluten and dairy, I realized that I stopped having colds. And when I *would* include gluten and dairy for an extended period of time, usually around the holidays or on a summer vacation, I would suddenly get a cold.

So rule number one for me is to avoid gluten and dairy as much as possible, indulging maybe once or twice a month, typically when I'm eating out with other people. It seems I can get away with this frequency without getting sick or a major skin breakout. There are countless amazing alternatives available in the grocery store or online retailers these days for people who are gluten- and dairy-free – from gluten-free pasta to oat milk and nut cheeses. Not all brands are created equal, though – so shop around until you find brands you enjoy.

However, you personally might not have a sensitivity to gluten or dairy at all. If you want to explore what foods you personally might be sensitive to, *Clean* by Dr. Alejandro Junger helped me, or you could talk to your doctor about getting an allergy test.

Rule number two for me is giving up alcohol, most of the time. The older I get, the more I find alcohol consumption to affect my sleep and overall well-being, including my mental health. It wasn't until I experienced how good I felt after extended periods without alcohol that I realized how depressed and anxious I would become in the aftermath of drinking and partying. After I got the alcohol out of my system, I felt so much clearer and happier. I also looked way better – less puffy and bloated. Now I'll sometimes have a glass or two of wine at a special celebration or holiday, but almost never if I have to work the next day. I have to stay sharp.

I also try to avoid ultra-processed foods that contain ingredients I can't pronounce, as well as canola oil and seed oils. I have found that weird chemical ingredients can make my mind race or cause skin breakouts, and that many types of oils, like canola, make my joints ache. (Olive oil, coconut oil, and avocado oil seem to be fine for me.) When I cut out canola oil and other random oils often found in low-quality processed foods, my knees suddenly felt good again, making it easier for me to be active.

And being consistently active has become really important for me, as well – I try to do something active, even if it's just a walk, five days a week. (Every day would be ideal, but I'm being a realist here.) I first realized the profound impact of exercise on my mental health when I escaped the Dave situation. Months after leaving my apartment and returning home to my parents, I was still incredibly depressed that Dave ended up being such a jerk, and that I would never find anyone – blah, blah, blah, you know how it goes. Instead of walking to work, I was driving to the office and back, and no longer getting any exercise at all. Then a friend of mine dragged me to a hot yoga class. I left feeling like I was walking on air. I just saw my situation completely differently and was finally like, "Ugh, who even cares about that loser? What else is going on in the world?" The experience was transformative.

I also now eat meat sparingly, usually only if I'm at a restaurant or at someone else's house and there are no fish or veggie options available. When that's the case, I just shut up, eat the meat, and enjoy it. If you're interested in learning more on why I avoid meat, the book *Clean* I've referenced in this chapter does a good job of explaining how conventional American meat is often pumped with hormones and antibiotics that can affect our health. However, I do still have a soft spot for bacon and will sometimes buy it at the grocery store, but only if organic is available.

Finally, I try to consume as many fruits and vegetables as possible. I do not fear fruit anymore. Let's be real, a banana was not causing my weight gain -- it was much more likely the wine I was drinking or the high-fat, processed snacks I would mindlessly eat at my computer. Fruit, even and especially bananas, is a great snack packed with vitamins and minerals to keep you healthy. (For more on the futility of fruit fear, check out Anthony William's book *Life-Changing Foods*.[26]) And I try to eat as many vegetables as I can at every

---

[26] Anthony William, *Life-Changing Foods: Save Yourself and the Ones You Love with the Hidden Healing Powers of Fruits & Vegetables* (Hay House LLC, 2016).

meal, even breakfast, to help crowd out the denser foods I consume, like grains, fish, and soy-free tofu.

I also throw in a vigorous vitamin regimen for good measure that includes vitamin B complex, vitamin C, zinc, lysine, and more unusual herbs like cat's claw, ashwagandha, and lemon balm. *Life-Changing Foods* by Anthony William also serves as a compendium of the benefits of these herbs, as well as other plants.

Ultimately, self-love means doing what is best for your health, and not just your palette. I find that after a day of eating very healthy, I sleep incredibly well and awaken feeling ready to take on another day. And when I do now indulge in richer foods or gluten and dairy, I almost feel like I'm hungover the day afterwards, even though I didn't have any alcohol.

One of my favorite hobbies these days is taking a craving for something indulgent as an inspiration to make a healthier version of it. Say I'm craving Chinese food. Do you know how easy it is to make gluten-free sesame noodles or gluten-free, dairy-free (and chemical-free) sweet-and-sour tofu? Recipes are just an online search away.

However, soul food is also a real thing. Sometimes there is nothing better than a freshly baked baguette with Brie cheese or chocolate spread, or pizza from your favorite neighborhood joint. But striking the right frequency of indulging without impairing your health is critical.

Conclusion

After making all these adjustments to my diet and activity levels, you would think I look even better now than I did in my 20s – when I was basically eating whatever I wanted and almost never exercised.

But… nope. Not even close.

I don't pretend to know the science behind why so many women start gaining weight in their mid-to-late 30s, especially if they're doing nothing differently from what they've always done, but I *do* know it's not fair. Especially when we finally get to a point in our lives where we can afford expensive restaurants and gourmet groceries. *That's* when we have to reel it in and start being more careful? Really?

HOWEVER – I *can* say that eating the way I do now and staying active has made me *feel* far better than I did in my 20s, when I was still getting colds six times a year and spending many of my best days hungover and depressed.

Am I a bit heavier today than I was then? Definitely. But if I had to choose between being skinny, sick, broke, and depressed versus being a little heavier but so much healthier, as well as financially and emotionally free – and certainly far better dressed – there's no contest.

I would undoubtedly choose where I am now.

6. COMMUNITY

NO LONGER AN OUTSIDER LOOKING IN

Now that we have covered how to build a solid foundation for your finances and well-being, we can start talking about a more fun, yet still tricky, part of life: relationships. And I don't mean romantic relationships. I mean friends and community.

When I was 28 and moved to the city where I currently live, I reconnected with some old friends from high school who had been living here for years. They were kind enough to introduce me to their local friends and include me at parties and in outings. I also leaned heavily on my sister and brother-in-law, who lived in the area. I joined dating apps as well and tried to arrange at least one date a week. Remember, I had to "get out there" and find The One! I also thought I might make some guy friends this way, which, in retrospect, is hilarious. I don't think I ever made one friend from a dating app.

And while the people I met through mutual friends were nice enough, we ultimately didn't have much in common and didn't enjoy a special connection. As a result, I remember walking through the city my first few years here, looking enviously at groups of people laughing over dinner at outdoor tables, drinking at rooftop bars, and lounging together in tree-lined parks. As much as I liked my new city, I still felt like an outsider.

I thought finding a boyfriend would fix this, so I doubled down on online dating. But other than a lot of first dates, a handful of second dates, and one or two five-to-six-month relationships, it just wasn't working. It wasn't until I reflected on how I had made my most meaningful connections to date that I finally got some clues on how to start building a better community.

A (broken) circle of friends

People often build community in their formative late teens and early 20s without even trying, whether in college, workforce training of some kind, or living with roommates for the first time. I was lucky enough to be one of these people, having collected what I thought to be a wonderful group of friends at the state university I attended. By my senior year, I was super tight with a core group of three other girls with whom I also lived, particularly my best friend Jess, and we had a couple different groups of guy friends with whom we would hang out and from which occasionally date.

As I'm sure many people can attest, in college, your friends become your family. Some of my happiest memories include my roommates and I going out for breakfast as soon as we woke up on the weekend so we could debrief and die laughing over whatever happened the night before. And then hanging around the house or running errands together.

I had broken up with my longtime boyfriend during my junior year (more on him later), and I was having a great time playing the field with my friends my senior year. Near the end of the school year, however, I started dating one of our guy friends, Steve. I unexpectedly ended up falling for him

– hard. This was complicated by the fact that I was leaving in May to live with my parents for the summer, five hours away, and in September would be attending graduate school halfway across the country.

Steve and I agreed that we would end things when I left in May and remain friends, and to just wait and see what life had in store for us, if anything at all. I admit that I was holding out hope that we would somehow get together when I finished school two years later.

After graduation, I went to live with my parents to work and save money for grad school, but I was still talking to my girlfriends – especially Jess – nearly every day. Steve and I were also texting often and writing on each other's "walls" (now timelines) on Facebook. So lame. My friends and Steve were all spending the summer at the beach, close to the university we went to, working during the day and going out every night. It sounded like so much fun; I was insanely jealous. My girlfriends also lived just two blocks away from Steve and his friends, and they all partied together often.

Can you see where this is going? I mean, if it were a movie, it would be so predictable. Well, six weeks after I left, Jess and Steve hooked up.

When Jess called me the day after it happened and confessed, I actually thought she was joking. There was just no way she could be serious. When she started to cry and weakly insisted that she was not, in fact, joking, I felt like someone punched me in the stomach. I remember I had just returned home from work and had picked up fast food from somewhere. I was eating my fries on my parents' back deck when I returned Jess's call. She sounded strange from the get-go. When she told me what happened, I hung up and promptly threw up. I then called her right back, shaking, and ordered her to tell me the details. I remember I kept hanging up and then calling her back to demand answers to more questions. *What happened? How far did it go? Do you even like each other? But...you're my best friend.* To her credit, she kept picking up and answering honestly, apologizing and crying the whole time. It was awful.

At the time I didn't know what devastated me more – that Steve, the guy I absurdly had seen as "The One," took an interest in my best friend, or that my best friend, who knew I still had strong feelings and hopes for this guy, hooked up with him. But in hindsight, nearly 20 years later, I can tell you it wasn't even close. Losing my best friend was by far worse.

To this day, I don't think I've ever experienced as much pain as I did at this time. I lost about twenty pounds, and I was thin to begin with. My parents were begging me to let them know why I was locking myself in my room and barely touching my meals, and I couldn't bring myself to tell them the whole story. They're Catholic, remember, and I thought they would look at me differently and tell me that this is what happens when you have sex before marriage, or at the very least, a long-term relationship. I had naively thought my relationship with Steve was so much more than a short-term hook-up situation, but I now know he didn't feel the same way. So for the rest of the summer while living with my parents, I had this horrible secret.

Everything was made unfathomably worse that the two people I cared about most at the time were the ones inflicting the pain.

My two other good girlfriends from college would occasionally call me and sympathize, saying how terrible it was and that they couldn't believe it. Apparently, Steve and Jess were still hooking up with each other, but he was also seeing other people. They said how distraught Jess was, how much she liked Steve but also missed me. At the time, this made me angry. *Oh, poor Jess? Whose side are you on?* But Jess and my other girlfriends were all still living together, and I was hours away, about to live in another world. Of course they would all stay close, and drift away from me. This situation just accelerated that inevitability.

Today if I saw Jess, I would hug her. She couldn't help how she felt for Steve and it probably seemed unfair that he was supposed to be off-limits when I wasn't even there. Even at the time, I understood that no one had technically done anything wrong, and I wasn't sure if I even had a right to be upset. (In retrospect, of course I did.) But really, weren't there any *other* cute girls and guys at the beach for them to pursue? Why did they have to complicate the perfect future I had envisioned and hook up with each other?

Because now our great circle of friends, my community and support system, was broken.

Grad school

So off I went to grad school, to a small but prestigious program thousands of miles away. It should have been one of the most exciting times of my life, but I was absolutely miserable, checking Jess and Steve's social media and instant messenger profiles every chance I got. Just torturing myself.

However, for the first time in my life, I also found myself surrounded by people with similar interests as mine: foreign languages and communications. There were about 14 other people in the program, and I clicked with many of them immediately. And I found myself, embarrassingly soon, spilling my guts to them about what happened to me over the summer. I confided in them during happy hours, while walking to class together, and while waiting in line to get burritos. I couldn't help it; everything I held in over the summer was bursting at the seams. I found my new friends' appalled reactions deeply gratifying, and soon everyone was making fun of how basic Jess and Steve were. The situation actually became a running joke in our group, and it felt good to laugh at them.

My new friends also dragged me out of my room to explore our new town, and we spent the next two years alternating between cramming for exams and staying out all night – with some road trips and other travel in between.

In the moments where I was alone, I still felt the pain. The rawness was easing bit by bit, but the grief was undeniably still there. When I was with my classmates, though, I was constantly amazed by how much we had in common, and how much we laughed together, which was even more than I did with my college friends.

Those two years became both the worst and best times of my life – up until that point, at least.

I wasn't jiving with everyone in my program, though. One girl in particular, Isla, was a thorn in my side. She would always roll her eyes when I spoke in class, and one day early on I overheard Isla tell someone I "was probably a sorority girl or something" and question why I was even there.

I was stunned and pretended I didn't hear her. Later I wondered, *Do I really seem like a sorority girl? What does that mean, exactly? How can I mention that I delivered greasy food in college?* I now wish I looked her in the eyes and asked her to repeat herself. I read somewhere that you should do that when someone says something rude. But with my luck, she would have been one of the few people to stare me in the face and shamelessly repeat it word for word, and I would crumble in terror. I have always hated confrontation. *Maybe I didn't belong here after all.*

Months passed from that moment and it became clear I wasn't Isla's only target. I had become friends with nearly everyone else in the program and soon learned that all of them had been personally insulted by her in some way. But when our professor acknowledged Isla's birthday in class one day and no one else said anything, I felt bad for her. She thanked the teacher with a tight smile and looked down at her desk. For the first time I saw how deeply lonely she was. Maybe she resented me and the other people in the program for being able to make friends so easily.

I remembered how lonely and isolated I had felt that past summer. In that moment I decided to give her another chance. I asked her where we were celebrating after class, and she looked startled. "That's okay, we don't have to celebrate," she said. No, let's go, I insisted. A couple of the other suckers in class rallied and joined in. Then the whole class ended up taking her to our favorite bar that evening. To be honest, everyone else's curiosity had just gotten the best of them, as I learned later. They didn't want to miss anything good. But we all had a great time. Isla and I even had a drunken heart-to-heart where I told her what I had overheard her say, and she was embarrassed and apologized.

Look, I'm not telling this story to make myself seem like a good person. I'm recounting it to illustrate how most groups or communities of people have at least one (or more) negative or socially awkward person who can make others feel uncomfortable or unwelcome, but we cannot let them discourage us from doing our thing. If the community is for you, you will experience an easy connection with most of its members. But rarely with all of them, and that is okay.

After two years of what felt like magic at grad school, my classmates scattered around the world. We were studying foreign languages, after all, so it was time to apply what we learned. I was one of the few who returned to her hometown to figure out next steps, as I was increasingly unsure that I wanted to stay on the foreign language path. Communications and marketing in English seemed to be more my thing.

I had no idea at the time how hard it would be to recreate the special feeling of community I had just experienced. As you now know, the friendships I made while dating Dave ended up being fleeting and were not that deep to begin with. Our common ground was just partying.

Fast forward to several years later when I moved to a bigger city and was trying to find my tribe by meeting friends of friends at parties and happy hours, and by online dating. But it just wasn't working. I literally wasted about four years of my life trying to force friendships with people I really had nothing in common with. When I left my job to go into consulting, it got even worse, as I was no longer surrounded by colleagues and office mates.

I finally realized that the last time I made real, magical connections was in grad school, when I was surrounded by people with similar interests.

So I pivoted. I joined a local book club and an international professionals' group. I started going to yoga more often and actually made an effort to chat with teachers and other students. I considered getting a part-time job in a restaurant, remembering some close friendships I had made in the past. I also joined a community service organization where the average age of members turned out to be about 65 years old.

Soon I was having belly laughs and effortless conversations again. I also received an exciting opportunity: an invitation to serve as a "Young Advisor" to the board of a prestigious fine arts organization in the city. Typically, board members of this organization donate tens of thousands of dollars (or more) to the organization every year. As a Young Advisor, I would offer marketing advice instead while enjoying the benefits of being affiliated with the organization. I was thrilled to accept.

One of the first events I went to was a beautiful dinner at a private dining club, followed by a behind-the-scenes tour of the organization's facility. At the dinner, I was seated between an elegant woman in her sixties who was a member of the board and a gentleman perhaps in his eighties, who used a walker to get around the room. I briefly panicked and wondered what on earth we would talk about. I was nervous to begin with, and wealthy older people weren't my usual demographic.

The gentleman, John, ended up being a total delight. We started talking about the city's arts scene, and I mentioned I had started my own consulting practice. (I was, and still am, always networking.) He praised my efforts and told me some amusing stories on how he started his own business back in the day. He also joked about his new assisted living facility and how coming out that night made him feel normal again.

At one point, the woman next to me, Babette, interrupted and started asking me probing questions. What was my connection to the organization? Why was I there? I explained how I was a Young Advisor, and she wanted to know when I joined, and who specifically on the board "brought me in" and why. I answered her questions to the best of my ability, telling her I assumed it was because of my marketing background and that the organization needed some help.

She said, "Well, if you're here because of your marketing background, maybe we should hear some marketing advice." I nervously obliged, telling her a few things I had come up with based on reviewing their existing marketing materials. John was looking at me encouragingly, nodding his head. Babette looked me up and down. "Thank you. I suppose you have paid for your supper after all."

I felt like I had been slapped. My face grew hot and I just knew I was beet red. I sort of nervously laughed, waited a beat, and then excused myself to go to the ladies' room. *Is it that obvious that I don't belong here?* I wanted to cry so badly but didn't want to mess up my makeup. I just wanted to go home and never see these people again.

I somehow pulled it together and made it through the rest of the evening, meeting other people during the tour after dinner. Most of the other people were much nicer than Babette – although there were a few other women eying me up and down, not bothering to introduce themselves. And I sure wasn't going to approach them. At one point I saw John leaving with another man, who was helping him navigate the stairs. We waved to each other and said goodbye. I turned back to the organization's executive director, Emily. She smiled broadly and said, "Thank you for making such a good impression on John. He told me he enjoyed speaking with you. He's one of our biggest donors."

Apparently, John had given the organization tens of millions of dollars over the course of his life, about $500,000 each year. And he was the kindest, most unassuming person I met that night.

When I got home later that evening, I immediately checked that year's record of financial support to see how much Babette had donated: $20,000. Interesting.

"Take the best and leave the rest." - Richard Branson
After that night, I was very tempted to quit my role

as a Young Advisor, to proverbially take my ball and go home. Even though there were no other incidents that evening, the shame Babette made me feel for my apparently obvious socioeconomic status went far deeper than when Isla called me a sorority girl. Maybe because Isla's insult implied I was privileged when I knew I wasn't, while I felt Babette saw me for who I was – a provincial imposter. All the women at this event had been dressed to the nines in tasteful but obviously designer clothing. I had worn a conservative, knee-length black dress from a mid-tier clothing chain and my only designer bag, the one from Maison Margiela with a beautiful vintage floral print. The one I bought when I landed my third client as a consultant.

But it obviously wasn't enough, and I suspected that my mannerisms and way of speaking just screamed middle-class to them. That, along with the fact that I couldn't make a donation large enough to make the official list of supporters. I skipped their next few events and considered officially stepping away.

Then I received a nice note from Emily, saying that they missed me at the last event and that she hoped I was well. She said the organization needed input from young people like me to improve ticket sales and to help secure the organization's future. She asked if she could send me free tickets to their next event; I could have as many as I wanted for me and my friends.

I was touched by the fact that Emily even noticed I hadn't been coming (more than 60 people attend those private events) and decided to give the organization another chance. I also realized that if all the good people in the world let people like Babette and Isla take over, it would become a very dark place indeed. What we need are more Johns and Emilys. I was reminded of the Amanda Gorman poem, "There is always light if only we're brave enough to see it, if only we're brave enough to *be* it." In other words, don't be an Isla or Babette. So I stuck it out, not wanting the Islas and Babettes of the world to win.

No longer an outsider looking in

My experience with this arts organization also brought me a new appreciation for the less "refined" or prominent groups of people entering my life, particularly friends I made as a volunteer in my community service group. What was probably my least conventionally "cool" group of friends had quickly become one of my favorites – and I now think they're cooler than anyone else.

These older and wiser women (because they *are* mostly women, for whatever reason) are hilarious, whip smart, and as kind as they are tough. Imagine about 20 Judge Judys or Dorinda Medleys sipping wine at the neighborhood diner. That's what our monthly meetings are like. If anyone wants to know what is really happening in this city, or needs some good life advice, they should consult these ladies. And for a good time, they should come to one of our epic trivia or drag bingo nights, where we raise money for underprivileged kids in our neighborhoods.

It also just feels good to contribute towards a higher common good, I'm not going to lie. Doing it as a team makes it a lot of fun and more gratifying. I'm still trying to work out how I feel about going to church – as a Catholic, it's complicated. But volunteering has shown me it is possible to give back and cultivate a spiritual life without subscribing to a specific religion. It also connected me with a community of inherently good people who want to help others – and who I believe would be there for me in a heartbeat if I needed them.

Of course, I also love my new friends in the

international relations world, who remind me a lot of my grad school classmates, and my yoga friends, with whom I have since traveled on retreats. I remain close with my grad school friends, as well, whom I try to see at least once a year through visits or trips abroad. Whenever I see them it's like no time has passed at all.

And I'm happy to report that when I walk through the city these days, I don't feel like an outsider looking in anymore. I just feel excitement for where I'm going.

7. FUN

UTTER FREEDOM TO DO WHATEVER YOU WANT

If work and health are the roots of living a fulfilling life, and community something that gradually stems after a bit of time and nourishment, the fruits are the fun: what you can now do with your robust income, well-being, and new friends.

The key point of the above being *you* can do whatever *you* want to do, not what your boyfriend wants to do, or your kids, or your parents. What. You. Want. To. Do.

One time I was getting coffee with two friends, Olivia and Kara. Olivia and I started talking about this documentary we both watched about the street cats of Istanbul, Turkey. All three of us were cat people, and Olivia and I told Kara she needed to watch the documentary immediately. It was excellent and she loved cats, so it was a no-brainer. But I'll never forget what Kara said. She just looked at us and sort of wistfully shook her head, saying, "Oh, I don't think Trevor will want to watch that."

Olivia and I, both single at the time, sort of did a doubletake. "What do you mean? Can't you watch it without him?"

Kara, who was married but didn't have kids yet, said, "Well, we only have one TV and I like to watch things I know he will also like. I would never hear the end of it if we watched what was basically a two-hour long cat video."

Olivia shot me a look, appearing a bit stung by this comment. She teased Kara, "Oh, so is that why you don't watch any *Real Housewives*? This whole time you've acted it like it was beneath you, but you actually just weren't allowed?"

This remark started an all-out argument, with Kara insisting that we just didn't understand because we were single.

Now, I know there are many married women out there who watch whatever the hell they want, with or without their partners. Whether they have more TVs or more time home alone – or maybe a more accommodating guy – they somehow make it work.

But apparently there exists a subset of couples out there who watch all TV shows and movies with each other all the time, and this came as a shock to me. Perhaps it is admirable that they try to spend most of their free time together and prioritize content that they will both like. However, I wonder if Trevor, whom I know to be a big sports fan, reciprocates by asking himself if Kara truly likes to watch sports with him all the time. Knowing Trevor, I doubt it.

Nothing irritates me more than when men belittle the interests or beloved pastimes of women, whether it be the types of media we consume, playing with cats, enjoying fashion, whatever. And in the meantime, they consider it perfectly fine to waste hours and hours watching sports, porn, and/or playing video games.

The truth is we all like to unwind in our own ways, and we should all be able to do so without shame or judgment. And this is one of the many perks of being single. If I want to watch a certain show, or read a certain book, or go to a certain place, I am going to do it.

But to be fair, there was once a time I sang a bit of a different tune.

When I was 32 years old, I was dating someone I met online. Let's call him Brad. I had just started consulting and only had one client, and I was deadass broke. I couldn't afford to do anything fun on my own or with friends. I was desperately searching for clients and didn't even want to think about dating until a friend suggested I get on the dating apps for the free meals. *Oh, good idea*, I thought.

So I rejoined the dating apps and decided to try something different this time: only date guys who appear to have money. In the past, I prided myself on only dating guys with whom I seemed to have chemistry, but, hey, that never seemed to work out. So I would try something new and see how it went.

Over the next month, I went out with about 11 different guys who appeared to be, if not rich, at least financially comfortable and in lines of work that seemed fairly lucrative.

And I kid you not, 10 out of the 11 were assholes.

These guys included a professional athlete who was over 30 minutes late and who was possibly the worst conversationalist I have ever met; an Ivy League guy in finance who didn't ask me a single question about myself; and a political commentator on a cable news network who seemed to take great pleasure in telling me how my political views were wrong.

However, the 11th guy, Brad, somehow ended up

being really nice. He was a vice president at a major corporation, and he courted me in a sweet, old-fashioned way. He would always take me out for an expensive dinner and always insisted on paying. He would find creative and romantic things for us to do, as well. About three months in, he told me he wanted to take me on a trip somewhere and asked if I had a passport. I did, but it was about to expire. "Better get it renewed," he told me.

So things seemed to be going really well and I was getting excited about where our relationship was going.

And then the holidays came.

Brad was about 10 years older than I, and he had already lost both of his parents to cancer. He also didn't get along with his sister, and he didn't have any other family. So as Thanksgiving approached and I was preparing to travel to my parents' house, I was panicking. Should I invite Brad home for the holidays? Was three-and-a half months of dating too soon? Wouldn't it be cruel to just leave the orphaned guy you're dating home alone on a major holiday?

I had formerly prescribed to the somewhat retro notion from *The Rules*[27] that women should introduce boyfriends to family only after the guy introduced her to his. But in this case, Brad didn't have any family to introduce me to. He had, however, introduced me to several of his friends, and he had later met some of mine, quite successfully.

I couldn't bear the thought of Brad spending Thanksgiving Day alone. I told myself to stop worrying about *The Rules* and invite him home for the holidays.

Big mistake.

When I invited him to Thanksgiving over dinner one

---

[27] Ellen Fein and Sherri Schneider, *The Rules: Time-tested Secrets for Capturing the Heart of Mr. Right* (Grand Central Publishing, 2007).

night, I could see him tense up immediately. He took a minute to answer and then said he enjoyed having a quiet holiday and to not worry about him. I said that I just thought it might be fun to have him, no pressure at all. But he shook his head.

I couldn't tell if he thought I was trying to push the relationship forward prematurely or if I was feeling sorry for him. So I immediately decided to let it go and changed the subject. I brought up an Indian restaurant that recently opened and suggested we try it sometime. He just made a face and shook his head. "I don't like that kind of food."

"Oh, ok," I said. "Have you tried Indian before? Maybe you just went to a bad place."

"I don't like it," he said slowly. "And the one paying gets to say where we go."

I felt like he slapped me. I was quiet for a minute, and then said, "I've tried to pay for dinner before, but you won't let me." This was true. It was also true that I held my breath until he said no. But I always had my credit card on standby in case he said yes.

"I would never let a lady pay for dinner," Brad said.

"So – what if the lady you're seeing wants to occasionally have some input? Is it then okay for her to pay?"

I was coming to the realization that Brad had never once asked for my preference or opinion in selecting the restaurant or activity for our dates. I had initially thought it romantic that he would choose the location and make all the arrangements, but with this new attitude of his, it felt less romantic and more chauvinistic.

"I don't know, Greta," Brad sighed. "If it's that Indian place or something weird, I'd rather not go at all."

I felt taken aback by this. How many times did I go to steakhouses or Italian places with him – neither my favorite –

and never say a word? To the contrary, I was always grateful for the meal and experience. Would this behavior never be reciprocated if I continued dating him? Would I never have Indian food again?

I also didn't know whether Brad's behavior was the real him finally rearing his ugly head or if it was caused by stress from my Thanksgiving invitation. Was he embarrassed that I felt sorry for him?

The rest of the dinner was strained, but we got through it. We still went back to his place, and I spent the night. The next morning I returned home, my mind racing.

Is this the norm in older and wealthier circles? I wondered, when I got back to my apartment. In my past relationships, even the more toxic ones, it always felt like we made decisions together on where we would go – and the guys usually still paid, although we were typically going to far more affordable places. I remember those guys asking me what kind of food I was in the mood for, or what movie I wanted to see. And looking at my parents' relationship, my dad, the breadwinner in the family, almost always defers to whatever my mom's preference is in a situation. But she is also considerate of what he wants, and they make those decisions together.

But with Brad and these higher-income guys I more recently went out with, one thing they all seemed to have in common was that they couldn't care less about what I wanted or how I felt. My opinion didn't matter, even to the only "nice one" of the 11, Brad.

If this scenario were to happen to me today, nearly 10

years later, I would have ended things with Brad that night, or at the very least, taken a major step back from the relationship. I would begin dating other guys and make more time for myself to do things I enjoyed.

But that's easy for me to say now, when I have the money and means to do fun things on my own. At the time I was dating Brad, this wasn't the case. And he was holding something over my head that I wanted very badly, much more than Indian food: a free trip.

Besides an annual beach trip with my family, I hadn't traveled anywhere cool since grad school. And I love to travel, whether it is just a few hours away by car or ten hours away by plane. I decided to hang in there and see what happened.

Thanksgiving passed and things with Brad more or less returned to normal. I never again mentioned him meeting my family, and he seemed to relax again. Then one night out at yet another fancy steakhouse, I mentioned that I just received my new passport in the mail.

"Oh, that's great," he said, taking a sip of his beer.

"Do you know where you want to go?"

"I'm thinking maybe Aruba. Have you been?"

"No, never. That sounds amazing."

We started talking about different places we had been to, and I told him how the only other continent I had visited is Europe. I also said how there are still so many places in America I'd like to visit, like Hawaii and many of the national parks out west.

"I've already been to Hawaii and the parks. Don't really need to go back," Brad said.

"Oh, I guess I'll do those with friends then," I said with a smile.

He snorted and said, "Oh, ok. If you ever find more clients."

That stung.

At this point, it had been about eight months since I started consulting, and I still only had one client. I had been confiding in Brad about my consulting journey the whole time we had been dating, and he had been a sympathetic ear. Or at least seemed to be.

"Wow," I said. "Thanks for the support."

He saw he made a misstep and backtracked. "How's the search going?"

"Fine," I said shortly. "Have some new leads."

"That's good." He ordered us another round of drinks. I shook off my annoyance and changed the subject.

A few days later, I was home and bored, aimlessly scrolling on my phone. I hadn't heard from Brad since our last date, which was unusual for him. I was debating whether or not I should text him first. But he was so old-school, and I didn't want to spook him again.

I decided to check his online dating profile, which I probably did about once a week, to see if he had any recent activity. We still had not had "the talk" about whether we would become monogamous, and we both still had our profiles up. Neither of us had updated them since we started dating, though, about four months earlier.

Until now. I saw that the day after I last saw him, Brad updated his profile to say how much he loves to travel and is "looking for a fun girl to take with him on a new adventure."

Motherfucker.

What the hell? I couldn't believe it. He already *had* a girl to take on his fucking adventure – me! Did he think I wouldn't see that he updated his profile? Did he *want* me to see it? Was this his twisted way of ending things with me?

I began to suspect that he smelled the desperation on me to take a trip with him. Maybe he saw how excited I was about it and wondered what would happen if he dangled a trip in front of other women. Would a hotter and more compliant one come running?

He better hope so – because there was no way I would go anywhere with him now.

Well, it turned out he wasn't planning on asking me, anyway. I wouldn't hear from him again – until two years later. *("Hey Greta, it's Brad from 2016!")*

I soon decided that this was my karma for dating guys for money. I was upset at first, but luckily Brad was easy to get over. To be honest, deep down I had known that Brad and I weren't a match. There wasn't any kind of deep connection, and we didn't have much in common. But we did have fun together and I enjoyed being courted – at least until the "courting" shifted into an unhealthy power dynamic.

Instead of swiping for new guys to treat me to trips and nights out, I decided to devote that time to finding more clients so I could afford to treat myself. I deactivated my dating profiles and started going to more in-person networking events, sending more cold emails to prospects, and asking people I've previously worked with for leads.

I also cut back on time spent with the friends I had during this period, as they were almost always drinking, and I couldn't afford to be hungover the next day. When I needed to get out of the house, I took a walk or did pay-what-you-can yoga instead. This was also the time where I started volunteering and reawakening previous interests of mine.

My life felt, at times, like a daily slog, but with a

growing number of moments where I met people I truly connected with or contributed to causes bigger than myself.

And lo and behold, after just a few months of all this, I landed my second client, a start-up who had been impressed with my local grassroot connections.

And then about two months after that, I landed my third and fourth clients, who had been referred by my second client.

And the money started to roll in.

As did my joy and relief.

Do you see what happened once I truly made my career a priority, took care of my health, and built up more community connections? These things, all interwoven, fed into each other, grew, and yielded fruit.

And now it was time to eat the fruit!

But don't do as I did and eat all the fruit at once. Save some of it, at least. I've already talked about the importance of building an emergency fund and investing as much of your disposable income as you can. Please always keep that in the back of your mind. But with that said, you only live once, and what is all this grinding for if not to enjoy at least *some* of the fucking fruit?!

And the fruits of your labor are not only money. They include time and freedom as well. Although I was now technically spending more time working, I was no longer spending so much time and emotional energy looking for clients and worrying about my future. That was so much more exhausting than just doing the work, and that was all time and energy I got back.

I also now had the freedom to do whatever I wanted with that time, energy, and money – and that was exciting.

But it was also a little scary. I was 33 at this point and totally single. I didn't really have a model of what a single woman should do with all this newfound money, time, and freedom. Everyone in my life and all the media I consumed told me I should be dating. But not one ounce of me wanted to go back to the grind of online dating. All online dating had produced for me was mostly terrible dates and half-hearted connections. I did not want to go back to spending my time that way.

It did not take me long to find other avenues, though. I decided to start with a trip.

Travel

I'll never forget the first trip I took once I finally found success as a consultant. Three friends and I went to Tulum, Mexico, to enjoy the beautiful beaches there, followed by Mexico City. An old friend of mine from grad school was living in Mexico City and met up with us there, showing us the sights and taking us to some of the best restaurants and bars I've ever been to.

It had been nearly 10 years since I last traveled internationally, and this trip was just what I needed after a decade of various emotional and financial struggles.

Magic was slowly, but surely, creeping back into my life.

Since going to Mexico, I've made several other trips to Latin America and Europe, as well as many more local trips within a few hours of where I live. I've done some things I never thought I would do, including hiking the Alps in France and Switzerland and seeing the Panama Canal. I've collected a number of favorite spots located just outside the city where I live, as well, where I like to hike and browse quaint shops and local farmer's markets.

One of the best parts of traveling, though, is the quality time you get with those you travel with. Some of the trips I took have been with friends from grad school, and some have been with groups of new people with whom I share a common interest. For example, the Alps trip was organized by my local yoga studio, so I got to know those people a lot better than I did previously by just attending classes. And I'm now planning a trip abroad with the Judge Judys and Dorinda Medleys from my community service group, which should be outstanding.

With that said, I'm also looking forward to taking a trip alone sometime soon. It can be difficult to agree on a destination with your friends, as well as an itinerary, and there is one place in particular where I want to return and do exactly what I want.

I can't wait.

Food

As I mentioned before, I love food, and when you love food and you're broke, it is very difficult to walk through a city packed with great restaurants. Remember when I felt like an outsider walking through the city and seeing other people out and about? That was partly because I hadn't found my tribe yet, but also because I simply couldn't afford to go out to dinner or a fun brunch, at least very often. And one of the best parts about living in a great city is the food!

Now I feel like I can finally fully participate in what my city has to offer. I try to limit dining out in pricier restaurants to once a week, just to be mindful of my spending, but this is enough to make me happy. (I order takeout or delivery from cheaper restaurants far more often.) And at this point I know all my friends' different tastes and dietary preferences, so when a new Middle Eastern or vegan place opens, I know just who to call to join me.

I also love to cook and can now enjoy more expensive and healthier ingredients. For example, one of my go-to dishes when I was broke was canned tuna over gluten-free pasta, with olive oil, lemon, and whatever dried herbs I had in the cabinet. (Honestly, this still sounds delicious to me.) Now I might swap the canned tuna for fresh or frozen fish (lobster if I'm feeling fancy), and add white wine, garlic, and fresh herbs to the sauce. I would also sauté a ton of fresh spinach or kale in the sauce so there is a 1:1 pasta to veggie ratio, helping to lighten things up for my 41-year-old body.

A great meal gives me so much joy. Oh, and just in case you're wondering, I order Indian at least once a month.

Live events

Something I also couldn't do as often as I would have liked when I was broke was see different kinds of live performances and events, whether music, comedy, theater, dance, and even sports. Sure, I could occasionally see a local band play for $10 or $20, but many of the most talented people (rightly) charge a premium to see them perform live. And seeing what they can do in person can be incredibly fun and inspiring.

Just this year, I've seen comedian Heather McDonald do her stand-up act, author David Sedaris read from one of his books, and the amazing cast of *Hamilton* retell history. I have two season tickets to the ballet and treat a friend to my extra ticket every time I go. And I almost always make it to a few professional sports games each year with family, especially my dad. (Pro tip: tickets to events make great holiday or birthday gifts for the people you love.)

Tickets to these kinds of events were at the bottom of my spending priorities when I didn't have money, but now, I appreciate going to them so much. They offer something special to look forward to and help create memories with the people I care about most.

SHOPPING

Of course, one of the most fun parts about being single with some money is the freedom to shop and build your wardrobe! However, do yourself a favor and try to keep your wits about you before you hit the check-out button.

As I've mentioned (several times now), one of the first things I bought when I finally had the means was a bag from Maison Margiela with a vintage floral print. It is a beautiful bag; when I first saw it, I just had to have it. However, I probably only use it once or twice a month due to its color story and delicate nature.

There were so many other things I needed before buying this beautiful yet utterly unsensible $2,500 bag. But alas, I was thinking with my heart, not my head.

Now, however, I keep a running list on my phone of the gaps in my everyday wardrobe, and I try to fill those before splurging on something that I won't wear as often. I also try to do my research so I buy something I love, and at the best price. For example, right now I desperately need a new black blazer. My old one has become quite worn in the elbows and it isn't as high of quality as I would like. So I have been researching the perfect black blazer on higher-end websites, researching different fabrics and checking the measurements of different styles to find the most flattering fit – and always keeping my eyes peeled for deals.

I also make myself stick to a certain clothing budget, because I could easily spend all of my income on shopping if I weren't careful. I also pay attention to what I'm wearing – and not wearing – from my existing wardrobe and adjust my spending as needed. For example, I have been wearing a lot of active and loungewear lately since I spend most of my days alternating between working from home and exercising. So, *do* I actually need that perfect black blazer after all? It's a staple, so I probably will get it, but I will hold off on buying any others until I get some mileage out of my new one.

Shopping is an ongoing game for me that keeps me endlessly entertained. And being single and childless gives me the financial freedom to be a little selfish and fully enjoy it. Should I feel bad about this? Not one bit. Couples get to enjoy perks specific to being in relationships (like watching all their TV shows together?) and aren't shy about talking about them, so we should freely enjoy perks specific to being single.

Exercise

Remember those pay what-you-can yoga classes I used to go to? I still go to some, but I'm proud to report that I have added some regular $18 sessions to the mix, as well. And my yoga studio has become one of my favorite communities, as I have now traveled with them a few times and have made real friends outside of class.

In fact, many people are finding community via their exercise routines, whether through yoga, run clubs, boot camps, and other group classes.

But honestly, one of my favorite ways to exercise these days is both free and solitary: hiking or just walking around the city while listening to my favorite podcasts. I have a growing number of (unhealthy?) parasocial relationships with podcasters whom I adore. Five years ago, I didn't really even know what a podcast was, but now they help break up my workday on the regular. They provide unique – and fun – perspectives on what's going on in the world.

Get reacquainted with yourself

Did you ever like to do something as a child that you would soon find embarrassing? I did. I loved to read from an early age, devouring a whole chapter book in less than a day. I remember going to the bookstore and getting four or five books, only to have them read in less than a week. My parents couldn't keep up with my reading habit, so I ended up re-reading each book we bought three or four times.

However, sometime around fifth or sixth grade, I realized that reading was associated with being a nerd. So I tried to hide the fact that I liked to read and actually even stopped reading so much, which I now find to be heartbreaking. I remember being a lot less happy when this happened. Reading would creep back in during summer and holiday vacations, but not often during the school year. Instead, I would try to talk on the phone more or go to the mall with friends so we could talk about nonsense and obsess about boys.

This pattern would go on, more or less, for decades. Then one day, after I began consulting, I heard that expression, "whatever made you weird as a kid will make you cool as an adult." This saying really resonated with me for some reason, and I decided to finally fully embrace my "weirdness." I joined a local city book club, and once I experienced more success as a consultant, I began ordering enough books to keep a certain original online bookseller in business.

I soon needed to buy more bookshelves to accommodate all of my new books, but that is another story for the next chapter.

Chances are that you also gave up a part of yourself somewhere along the way, whether to fit in or please someone else in your life. Try reawakening this part of yourself and see what happens.

8. HOME
THE LUXURY OF LIVING ALONE

When you have a blossoming career, active wellness regimen, busy community life, and fun social calendar, you will often get exhausted from all the coming and going. And let's be honest. Other people can drain you of your emotional and mental energy, as well. Frankly, there are moments where I feel like everyone I know is annoying me – colleagues, friends, family – and I just don't want to deal with anyone.

Enter my home, my sanctuary. I think my absolute favorite time in the world is when I come home to a clean house, take a long shower or bath, order takeout, and binge a new show or read a book. Even when I'm on a fancy trip somewhere and am having the time of my life, after a few days, I inevitably start noticing how little things just don't measure up to being at home, where I designed everything to be just how I like it. The water pressure in the hotel will be a little too strong, the mattress just a bit too soft, or I weary of spending every waking moment with my travel companions.

There really is no place like home.

For the first 28 years of my life, I lived with family or

roommates – minus that disastrous two-year stint from Chapter 4. And during those two years, from ages 24 to 26, I *hated* living alone. But I think that's largely due to my mindset at the time. Because I was so miserable dating Dave, when I was alone in my apartment, I would just ruminate on all the things going wrong in the relationship. I wasn't doing things I enjoyed: experimenting in the kitchen, reading interesting books, or having a spa night. I was too broke to have cable, and streaming services weren't a thing yet. (Netflix was still in its DVD infancy.) My friends were also Dave's friends, so I felt like I couldn't confide in anybody. Instead, I was usually worried about the latest thing I did to make Dave upset and how I could make it up to him. Sad, I know.

So, for a while, I thought living alone just wasn't for me. But it turns out, in my case at least, I just wasn't doing it right.

The next time I lived alone, at age 29, in the new house I bought, I wasn't under the spell of an asshole, and I *loved* living alone. I loved being able to make a mess in the kitchen and leave it until the next day without upsetting anyone else. I loved not having to schedule time in the bathroom to get ready. And I loved having people over and entertaining, whomever and whenever I wanted – and also not having to entertain other people's guests.

The closest I ever came to living with a boyfriend was when I was 20 years old, between my sophomore and junior years at college, when I was spending the summer in a beach house with my friends. In the beginning of the summer, my boyfriend at the time, Adam, was at the house so often that my roommates joked about charging him rent. (In retrospect, they probably weren't joking.)

Adam, to this day, is probably the most objectively good-looking guy I have ever dated. He is also an incredibly good person: kind, honest, generous, and friendly to everyone he meets. He has a great sense of humor and is quick to make a joke at his own expense. And Adam treated me like gold for the entire year-and-a-half we dated and is to this day the standard to which I hold every other guy I date – along with my dad, that is.

That summer, however, I could not stand him.

I'm not sure what it was exactly. Yes, I was seeing him almost every day, but I saw him often during the school year, too. We worked together at an on-campus restaurant and more or less merged our two groups of friends, whom we partied with and hung out with in our down time. The only nights I didn't see him were the ones where I had to study – and let's be honest, I wasn't studying as much as I should have been.

I think the difference was that Adam didn't spend a ton of time in my dorm room, which was tiny and shared with a roommate. We would often be out and about or hang out at his house, where he had his own room. When I finally got a house that summer, however, that flipped the script.

Without the burden of classes or a full-time job, it seemed Adam was always just *there*, in my house. Lounging on my couch, leaving dishes in the sink, and always wanting to chat. When I wouldn't feel like talking, he would ask me over and over again, "What's wrong?" *"Nothing -- I just have nothing to say."* "There's something wrong," he would insist.

This happened seemingly every day.

Then there were my roommates. A week or two into the summer, I started noticing when they would roll their eyes at each other when Adam would come over, or when he would do or say something mildly annoying. Which was often.

At one point, I remember locking Adam and myself

in my room and telling him that he couldn't come over so much; it was annoying the other girls. He scoffed at this, saying I paid rent and was allowed to have guests, just like they did. *Yeah, but theirs don't come over every day,* I thought. "Plus, they love me!" Adam said.

Finally, Adam went on vacation with his dad to Europe for two weeks. And let me tell you – those were by far the best two weeks of the summer. My roommates and I had a ball going to the beach, binge watching *Sex and the City* for the first time, and throwing a party without any of our boyfriends there. It wasn't until Adam came back and started coming over every day again that I realized how much more fun I was having without him.

In fact, when he returned and came through the door with a big smile on his face, it felt like a rain cloud covered our joyful little house. His presence really put a damper on things.

I locked him in my room again and was trying to communicate to him that he couldn't come over as much. I don't remember the words I was using, but he just wasn't accepting what I had to say. He kept shaking his head, saying stuff like, "It's normal for couples to spend most of their time together. That's what people in relationships do." I was getting frustrated and at one point, screamed into a pillow. He stared at me, shocked, and one of my roommates knocked on the door to make sure I was ok.

I called to her that I was fine, and Adam shook his head at me, saying, "You're not fine. I've been telling you that something has been wrong all summer."

Yeah, you're what's wrong, is what I wanted to say, but I couldn't bring myself to do it. *I'm in love with him,* I reminded myself.

At least I *was* in love with him – at first. When we first started dating, I liked him so much it scared me. I thought he was "The One," for sure, and for the first year we dated, the thought of us ever breaking up would make me sick.

Then that summer happened. And the combination of his stifling presence and my friends' reactions to it was making me feel increasingly claustrophobic.

"Listen, my roommates and I really need some girl time. There are certain things we can't talk about with a guy around – even one we love as much as you. I really need you to give us some space. Or else we need to break up."

His jaw dropped. "What the fuck, Greta? You can't just go around saying stuff like that." He seemed shaken.

"Well, you have to actually listen and accept what I'm saying. I don't care what most other couples are doing. This is what I need."

"Is it what *you* need or what your friends need? There's a difference."

"It's what I need." But he did have a point. Would I feel as suffocated by him if my friends had been more accepting? Maybe not as much, but I do think I would have gotten to this point, regardless.

Adam and I didn't last long after that summer. Even though he was seemingly the perfect guy, I realized that I was enjoying my time far more without him around. We were both young and still growing into who we would become. But aren't we always still growing into who we will become?

Fast forward 20 years later, I still haven't met a guy I liked enough to want to share my home with him. And to be honest, at this point, even if I were dating a guy I really liked, I don't think I would want him to move in.

The thing is, I have spent a lot of time and money on

my home over these years making everything just how I like it, and it would take a very special guy that I trusted very much to share it. I am still in the duplex I bought when I was 29, but I have since moved from the property's one-bedroom apartment unit into the three-bedroom apartment unit. I also made major renovations in both units, hiring contractors to install central air, brand-new kitchens, bathrooms, appliances, flooring, a fresh coat of paint – and lots of bookshelves.

A lot of people think they don't have the money needed to make renovations like this, but I did mine without putting any money down at all. I would encourage you to talk to a mortgage broker to see what they can do and shop around until you find one who really listens to what you want and will move mountains to make it happen.

I found my broker back when I first bought my house, and he was so good that I refinanced with him twice over the years, even when he had changed companies. I literally tracked him down on a career networking site so he could help me out.

"But, wait," you might be thinking. *"What does refinancing even mean?"* I really had no idea what it meant before my parents and brother-in-law explained it to me, so I will explain it here in case it is helpful.

I first met my mortgage broker 12 years ago when I was trying to buy my house for $203,000. He walked me through different types of loan programs available to me, and it became clear that the Federal Housing Administration (FHA) loan was the one for me. An FHA loan allowed me to put down only 3.5 percent in cash, or about $8,000. The loan would be repaid in monthly installments for the next 30 years – aka my mortgage. My mortgage was initially about $1,400 a month, which included property taxes and insurance.

However, as is often the case, during negotiations with the seller of the house, we hit a few snags. First it was over who would pay for closing costs – there was no way I could afford them, so the seller finally agreed to pay them. Then the FHA inspector announced that a termite treatment would be needed before the deal could move forward. The seller said since he was paying for closing costs, there was no way he would pay for the termite treatment, which was around $800.

At this point, my entire life savings was already going towards the down payment of the house, and I literally did not have any other penny to my name. My parents were not yet fully on board with the idea of my buying a house (they didn't think I was ready), so they were not about to lend me the money. I emailed my mortgage broker about my predicament and was about to resign myself to not buying the house after all.

Then my mortgage broker called me a few hours later and told me some of the best news of my life: he got his mortgage company to agree to pay for the $800 termite treatment! I was in shock. Why would they do something like that? It turns out they would be making way more in interest from me over the life of the loan that covering the $800 termite payment was worth it to them.

I had not asked for them to pay for the treatment and had no idea that it was even a possibility. This is why I recommend always being honest with your broker and telling them your actual financial situation, no matter how embarrassing. The good ones have many tricks up their sleeves to make a deal happen.

About six years after buying the house, I was getting

the itch to renovate and asked my brother-in-law for advice. He told me I could possibly refinance my house to pay for renovations and that I should talk to my mortgage broker. I tracked down Nick, my mortgage broker, and asked him to help. He suspected that the value of my home had gone up, as my neighborhood had greatly improved. More restaurants and businesses were being built in the surrounding blocks, and more people were buying and renovating properties that had fallen into disrepair.

He decided to get my property appraised, which meant he sent someone over to inspect my house and estimate its new value. It turned out he was right. The value had gone up dramatically, to about $400,000, an increase of about $200,000.

That meant his company could tap into the $200,000 increase in value to give me another loan to make renovations, which I would pay back monthly with my existing mortgage. But I needed to make sure I didn't take out too much money or else I wouldn't be able to afford my new monthly payment.

I asked different construction contractors for estimates on how much it would cost to make the renovations I wanted. I went with the one who had the best references and who also offered the best deal – about $100,000. I then asked my mortgage broker how much my new monthly payment would be if I took out an additional $100k – and he said about $2,100 a month.

This was a significant jump from $1,400 a month, but by this point I was earning significantly more money than I had been. I would also be able to charge a higher price for the apartment I rented out, as it would have more amenities like central air, a dishwasher, an in-unit washer and dryer, and beautiful finishes in the kitchen and bathroom.

In fact, when the renovations were completed, I was able to rent out the one-bedroom apartment for about $1,400 a month, which is $400 more than I got for the *three*-bedroom unit when I first bought the property.

And that meant I was only paying about $700 a month of my own money to live in a beautiful three-bedroom apartment in one of the ten largest cities in America. I currently enjoy the largest bedroom I've ever had, along with a guest bedroom, an office/gym, and all the aforementioned amenities of the other apartment. I even have a cute little deck out back.

I made all of these renovations with zero money down. I even got to save a little money by skipping two mortgage payments due to the date we signed the final papers – you could ask your mortgage broker to arrange this for you, as well.

Over time, I have met so many people older than I – both men and women – who wish they made an investment like this, especially so early in life. Because if and when I do want to leave this house one day, I could keep the property and rent out both units, which would pay the entire mortgage and make an additional profit. And when the mortgage is completely paid off, about 24 years from now, the rent payments will be almost entirely profit (after property taxes and insurance), which makes for a very good retirement plan. Or I could make a larger lump sum by selling the property, which will (hopefully) have further appreciated in value.

Now with all this said, the renovation process was at times brutal. I started the process at the very end of 2019, which meant the majority of the work was done during the pandemic. Not fun. The number of permitting delays and supply shortages we went through was incredibly challenging. But it also meant my money went further than it would now, as construction costs have gone up a bit since the pandemic started.

Let me tell you – if I could manage renovations on my own during a pandemic, so could you. And it was so worth it.

I wanted to spell out how refinancing a house works because I don't think a lot of women ever picture themselves buying a home on their own, let alone renovating one. Until the age of 28 or so, I always thought I would meet a guy first, get serious, and then buy a home together – or I'd just move into his house. I didn't think I needed to put the cart (the house) before the horse (the guy), so to speak.

But as you can see, that isn't the path my life took. And I didn't want to waste years of my life renting when I could be building equity in a house. You don't have to, either. And even women whose lives do follow a more conventional path could find this advice helpful if their marriages end prematurely – since about half of them inevitably will.

Going through property negotiations and learning how to refinance to renovate was liberating for me. I did not have to live with a man to feel like an adult. I did not have to believe that my life had begun only when I finally met The One.

I could forge ahead and build an amazing life for myself – starting with a beautiful home.

Buying a house and fixing it up can seem daunting, like climbing a mountain, but for me, it helped just taking it one step at a time. The path would soon unfold.

But maybe owning a property just isn't for you. I totally get that – the maintenance and responsibility isn't for everyone, although, for me, it really wasn't as bad as I feared. I haven't had to repair anything since my current renter moved in six months ago, but there have been months in the past – usually between tenants – where I have had several major repairs to make. It all evens out in the end.

However, all single women, regardless of whether they own their home or not, can certainly enjoy the luxuries of living alone. They include:

- Not having to clean up after anyone else.
- Having your bed to yourself. And not having to have sex if you don't feel like it.
- Eating whatever you want, whenever you want. You don't feel like you have to make dinner every night.
- Decorating however you want, and not having to accommodate "a man cave."
- Not having to talk when you don't want to.
- Getting a pet and spoiling it rotten.
- Not having to constantly navigate another person's negative moods.

I also hire a cleaning service to do a deep clean of my house once a month and enjoy doing so without judgment (I'm looking at you, Chris from Chapter 2). It takes them about four hours to perform a deep clean and costs $125. Since I can earn approximately $400 to $800 in that same window, it is far more worth my time to contract the deep cleaning out to someone else. I do a reasonably good job of maintaining it myself until their subsequent visit. Since a tidy home equals a tidy mind to me, this is money incredibly well spent.

Conclusion

Life is comprised of little and big pleasures, as well as little and big disappointments. Having a home you love can help ease the pain of the tough moments and can make the good ones seem even better.

For years I chased fulfillment by partying and dating and searching for The One, but creating a beautiful home that I love has ultimately brought me more peace and happiness than any of those things. I still experience moments of boredom or thinking "is this all there is?" But that is a part of life. I can practically guarantee those moments also abound in marriage. It is in those moments where spirituality can help, or proactively scheduling more fun and community outings.

But once I'm out, I almost always can't wait to go home.

9. DATING – THE FIVE COMMANDMENTS

When you get busy building a full and fulfilling life on your own, your attention naturally shifts from finding a partner to focusing on more things you can control. However, there's a big chance you might still want to date, especially if you're on the younger side. As women, we tend to have a lot of love to give. But if redirecting this love to yourself and to those with whom you share non-romantic relationships isn't enough, then of course, go forth and date. But for the love of God, please take a look at some rules and boundaries I have created for myself over the years and consider trying them out for yourself.

Please note that my rules are different from the classic dating book *The Rules* by Ellen Fein and Sherrie Schneider. With that said, I was a student of *The Rules* for most of my dating career and I would personally summarize them by saying they're like "playing hard to get." They have often worked for me in the short-term (Brad) and sometimes in the long-term (Adam), and they can do a decent job of filtering out toxic men. Definitely worth a read.

However, my rules have a different objective from *The Rules* book. *The Rules* seeks to get you a husband. That is their end goal. My rules seek to protect you physically, emotionally, and mentally while dating – especially online dating – and otherwise living your life.

With that said, however, I personally find that the rules on the following pages can often have the side effect of making certain men crazy about you, because you remain so unbothered by them.

And without further ado, here are my rules – all five of them.

1. Thou shalt NOT consult psychics

When you're single and the future is uncertain, it can be very tempting to consult a psychic on your romantic life. I am personally guilty of this and know countless other women who have done this, as well. The age of social media has made this even easier and more commonplace. Haven't we all paused while scrolling to watch a social media psychic go live?

A good friend of mine, Lauren, once consulted a psychic about her dating life and received a very specific description of her future husband – six foot three, reddish brown hair, green eyes. The psychic also said he would be significantly older than she and would be very smart, speaking several languages, with a high-paying job that required some domestic travel, and three sisters. The psychic said he also had a second home of some sort on the West Coast, and that Lauren would meet him during May of the following year.

Well, during May of the following year, Lauren met someone with that very description – her new boss. Who was married. My friend tried to tell herself that he couldn't be The One, but she didn't really believe it. She spent a whole year looking for clues that he and his wife were about to split up, while half-heartedly dating other people. After a year of this, she finally got the message that he and his wife were never going to break up, as much as he may have complained about her at the office. So Lauren moved on. But she literally had to get another job to fully break herself of the delusion.

I personally have a theory that this psychic did "see" Lauren meeting her boss and sensed that she would enter into some sort of contract with him. But the psychic misinterpreted what she saw, and instead of a marriage contract, it was actually a *business* contract. Who knows?

Whatever the case, this rule is not about whether or not psychics are legit. It's about protecting your sanity and living your life authentically. I do not believe it is healthy to get ideas planted in your head by a psychic which may artificially influence how you live your life. Had Lauren never gone to that psychic, she probably never would have caught feelings for her boss, and she wouldn't have had false hope that he would soon be single. She would not have wasted that year of her life and would have had her eyes open to other opportunities.

The psychic I personally saw told me I would be married with two kids by the age of 37, and I most definitely was not. Please do not waste your time and energy on psychics.

2. Thou SHALL consult the internet

Even at its best, dating can be annoying, but at its worst, it can be putting your life at risk. I once went out with a guy, a college professor, who I strongly suspect smashed my parents' car windshield when I refused a second date with him. I had made the mistake of letting him take me home after our first date. I assumed that since he was an esteemed professor at the local university, he had to be a pillar of society, right? (As the police would tell us later, that type of man can often be the worst.)

Clearly, I was wrong. So now this guy knew where I lived, and the day after I said no when he asked me out again, the windshield of my parents' car, safely parked in the driveway, got shattered overnight. Nothing like that has ever happened in my parents' neighborhood, before or since.

And then there's a friend of mine who once saw a guy she went out with on the news, being arrested – for being a serial killer.

We met both of these guys online, and our dates were in public places – thank goodness – but our stories still could have ended tragically. And this kind of casual meet-up has been totally normalized in the age of online dating.

So, my second rule for dating is to do my homework on any guy I have a date with. If I were to meet him online, I ask him for his full name, where he works, and for all his social media handles so I can research him and basically conduct my own background check. (If he asks for my full information, I say no, citing female privilege. And if *he* says no, then I say no to the date.)

If I meet him through a friend, even better. I can hold my friend's feet to the fire and ask for any and all information they might have on him. How did they meet and when? When was his last serious relationship? Why did it end? What has been my friend's personal experience been with this guy?

Pro tip: ask for this type of information AFTER you have been chatting with the guy for a while. That way you can catch him off guard and see if his online presence verifies all the stuff he's already told you – or if he is a big fat liar. For example, is he really a vice president at that company or is he is a junior associate? (The position doesn't matter; the lie does.) And who is that woman commenting on so many of his posts? A current girlfriend, situationship, or even his wife? If you don't care about seeming crazy, DM her and ask. (Just joking…or am I? What do you have to lose, really?)

A major red flag is if he has no internet fingerprint at all, if the guy has no social media accounts or online evidence of working where he says he works. Another is having no social media followers or having followers that are mostly bots. Or maybe he follows a lot of scantily clad women. Chances are you have an idea of what a normal guy's social media accounts should look like. See how he measures up.

With this said, please note that I had obtained all this information from the psycho college professor ahead of time. He gave me his full name and profession, and I confirmed this information on the university website. His social media also appeared normal. But he still ended up being a freak. So always proceed with caution – and never get in a car with someone you just met or let him know where you live.

Also, be smart about the information you disclose on your own online dating profiles. Keep your own social media accounts private if you can. One guy I went out with admitted to me that he found my professional profile before we met up – he just searched my first name, city, and where I went to college, which was stupidly on my dating profile. My professional page popped right up. I would now never include personal info on a dating profile, and I have made all of my social media accounts private.

Screening a guy's online presence is a great way to filter the worst ones out of your lineup, although it's still not a golden ticket. If the guy you're talking to is right for you, he will understand and humor you in this exercise. In fact, I have found that doing this made guys seemingly respect me more.

The good ones, at least.

3. No sex before monogamy

This rule is from the great and underrated Patti Stanger, also known as *The Millionaire Matchmaker*. No. Sex. Before. Monogamy.

This rule only applies if you are looking for a boyfriend or husband. If you are looking to "just have fun," that is totally cool and you don't have to follow this rule. (Hell, you don't have to follow any of these rules if you don't want to.) But make sure you're not kidding yourself. Many women like to say they're "not looking for anything serious," while secretly hoping a situationship will turn into something serious. Remind yourself that movies like *No Strings Attached* or *Friends with Benefits* are just that, movies. Life is not a romantic comedy. Many men tend to take what you say at face value and will think they hit the jackpot if you say that you're not looking for anything serious.

Ask yourself what you truly want and make sure your actions align with it. If what you truly want is a committed relationship, it can be torture to sleep with a guy and have him never call you again. Or to have him treat you like an option, while you're regularly checking his online profiles, wondering if he is dating other people, and trying to play it cool.

Men have gotten so spoiled that many *expect* or even feel entitled to sex if they make it to a third date. Why have we as women allowed society to normalize this? After just three dates, that guy has not done nearly enough to earn our trust and the right to our bodies.

On one third date I was on, the guy definitely seemed to think that something big was going to happen. We made out after dinner and he asked if I wanted to go back to his house. I gently told him I don't hook up unless I'm exclusive with a guy, to avoid STDs and "other complications." He seemed surprised by this but not put off. In fact, he seemed to think it made sense. Two dates later, he said he wanted to be exclusive. I said it was still a little fast for me, and that I wanted us to take our time. He sort of laughingly sighed and said, "Ok, fine."

The next couple of weeks, he went out of his way to show me how much he liked me and cared. We soon did the deed and ended up dating for six months before I broke up with him.

Listen, I am well aware that he could have broken up with me the day after we hooked up. That's always a risk. But that would be on him. At least we would have been communicating what we each wanted and would be on the same page, instead of us hooking up and leaving me wondering if and when we were ever going to have "The Talk" – while he's likely out chasing other women.

Had I always done this and told various jerks I dated that I wanted to wait until we were exclusive, I strongly suspect I never would have heard from many of them again. And that would have been a good thing – they wouldn't have wasted my time and energy.

4. No marriage or contracts of any kind before three years

Finally, before marrying a guy or even entering into a business relationship with him – or anyone, for that matter – I would require myself to have known him for at least three years. I wouldn't have to necessarily date the guy for the full three years – years spent as friends count, too.

I cannot tell you how many romantic, platonic, and business relationships I have been in over the past 20 years where, after knowing someone for one-and-a-half to three years, their mask was lifted – and I found myself dealing with someone who ultimately couldn't be trusted. Or even an outright narcissist or sociopath.

One woman I almost went into business with turned out to be completely two-faced, saying one thing to my face and something else to our potential clients. A former friend took a business idea I told him in confidence and tried to frame it as his own to a potential investor. A former colleague took something I said in jest and twisted it to our boss.

All three of these people were very fun, charismatic, and seemingly kind – people I was excited to be friends with, but by whom I ended up being very disappointed.

Something all three of them had in common, however, is that they couldn't hide who they really were for long. The mask came off usually between year one and three of our friendships. These people just couldn't help themselves.

On the other hand, I still have friends from decades ago, even from high school, that I would trust with my life. Do these people sometimes make mistakes? Of course, as do I. But we usually at least have good intentions, and we both do our part to get the friendship back on track when needed.

Think of all the nightmare divorces and lawsuits in the world. Do you really want to be a party to any of that? Often just knowing the person for a longer period of time – at least three years, in my experience – would help you see their true colors and weed out bad apples.

So I urge you, before tying yourself contractually with another person, whether it be for marriage, a home, or a business, please take your time and get to know that person well.

5. Follow the tenets of this book

The fifth and final rule is to simply follow Chapters 4-8 of this book. When I finally made my career, health, community, fun, and home priorities in my life, I no longer had any time or patience for a partner who doesn't share those priorities or have my best interests at heart. It also means I am organically putting myself in places to meet like-minded men, whether at business or community events, while working out, or traveling. I have met many men this way – with far better results than online dating. (At least for me – I do know several couples who met online and went on to be married.) My parents also love to remind me that they first met in church.

Following the principles from this book has also made me a much more attractive person from the broke, sick, lonely person I once was. I am so much happier and more confident now, and that confidence often naturally leads to meeting other happy, confident, and normal people.

Remember: a wedding is not the prom; it is the first day of a lifelong partnership with someone. These rules, while no guarantee, can help filter out the men who do not have your best interests in mind – and possibly even help you find The One.

10. CONCLUSION

There's a trend going around social media where the younger version of a person meets themselves in present day, and the present-day version tells the younger version what life is like for them now. Sometimes the younger self is disappointed, and sometimes they're pleased or intrigued.

I won't bullshit you. The younger version of me would probably be disappointed that I didn't end up the modern-day version of a fairytale princess – married off to a handsome and wealthy finance guy or business magnate.

However, I like to think that if the future, *older* me met myself today, she would tell me how relieved and proud she is. Of how hard I've worked so she can retire early, of how I've protected and nurtured my body, and of how many rock-solid friendships and community connections I've built over time. Of how many memories and enjoyable moments we've experienced together.

I personally believe that one of our main purposes in life is to become the best, most balanced versions of ourselves we can be. For men, maybe that means becoming more sensitive or detail-oriented. For women, maybe it means becoming stronger or taking more calculated risks. And for all of us, maybe it is becoming more compassionate towards each other and learning to make compromises without compromising ourselves.

For as much as I've demonstrated the shortcomings of dating, there *are* a lot of Good, and even Great, Guys out there, too. I'm lucky to have several in my life – my father, brothers, and friends. And one thing they have shown me is that if I'm not getting the same unconditional love I get from them in a romantic relationship, then I don't want that romantic relationship.

And let's not forget all the unconditional love from the amazing *women* in my life – my mother, sisters, female friends – which is so often taken for granted in our society. Why is that, anyway? Why do we so often put a premium on conditional love from loser men who don't even deserve us, and not on the love from the many women who love us no matter what, every day?

If these undeserving men want the benefits of being with a woman – and there are many benefits – they are going to have to step up to the plate. They are going to have to learn to be kind, to be giving, and to be considerate. Otherwise, we don't need, or want, them.

Because, as a crescendo of female voices is attesting, women are not usually leaving relationships to be with another man. Instead, we are leaving for ourselves. We are leaving for our peace. We are leaving for our well-being.

We are leaving to live a singular life.

For more stories, secrets, and recommendations from the author, Greta Booth, sign up for her free newsletter at asingularlife.com or follow @asingularlifebook on Instagram and TikTok.

Bibliography

Argov, Sherry. *Why Men Love Bitches: From Doormat to Dreamgirl—A Woman's Guide to Holding Her Own in a Relationship* (Adams Media, 2002).

Bernstein, Gabrielle. *The Universe has Your Back: Transform Fear to Faith* (Hay House, 2025).

Brunsman, August. "Why Gen Zers Are Single—and Happy About It." Psychology Today, August 2024, last accessed June 13, 2025, https://www.psychologytoday.com/us/blog/talking-apes/202408/why-gen-zers-are-single-and-happy-about-it.

Bushnell, Candace. *Sex and the City* (Grove Press, 2011).

Byrne, Rhonda. *The Secret* (Fang Zhi/Tsai Fong Books, 2007).

Cain Miller, Claire. "Young men embrace gender equality, but they still don't vacuum," *New York Times*, February 11, 2020, https://www.nytimes.com/2020/02/11/upshot/gender-roles-housework.html.

Ciciolla, Lucia and Suniya S. Luthar. "Invisible Household Labor and Ramifications for Adjustment: Mothers as Captains of Households," Sex Roles 81, 467–486 (2019), last accessed June 13, 2025, https://link.springer.com/article/10.1007/s11199-018-

1001-x.

Cox, Daniel A. "Is Marriage Better for Men?" American
    Survey Center, November 30, 2023, last accessed June
    13, 2025,
    https://www.americansurveycenter.org/newsletter/i
    s-marriage-better-for-men/#.

Dijkstra, Pieternel, Dick P. H. Barelds, Sieuwke Ronner, and
    Arnolda P. Nauta. "Personality and Well-being: Do
    the Intellectually Gifted Differ From the General
    Population?" Advanced Development 13 (2012), last
    accessed June 13, 2025,
    https://www.proquest.com/openview/e3172a3e4f5fb
    6de3b69bb39925f9abf/1?pq-
    origsite=gscholar&cbl=28640.

"Domestic Violence Statistics," National Domestic Violence
    Hotline, last accessed June 13, 2025,
    https://www.thehotline.org/stakeholders/domestic-
    violence-statistics/.

Fein, Ellen and Sherri Schneider. *The Rules: Time-tested
    Secrets for Capturing the Heart of Mr. Right* (Grand
    Central Publishing, 2007).

Galloway, Scott. *The Algebra of Wealth: A Simple Formula for
    Financial Security* (Portfolio, 2024).

Gurley Brown, Helen. *Sex and the Single Girl* (Barricade
    Books, 2003).

Harvey, Steve. *Act Like a Lady, Think Like a Man, Expanded*

Edition: What Men Really Think About Love, Relationships, Intimacy, and Commitment—Relationship Advice from a Man's Perspective (Amistad, 2014).

"How to Sell on Amazon: a guide for beginners." Amazon, last accessed on June 13, 2025, https://sell.amazon.com/sell.

Junger, Dr. Alejandro. *Clean: The Revolutionary Program to Restore the Body's Natural Ability to Heal Itself* (Harper One, 2010).

Kiyosaki, Robert. *Rich Dad, Poor Dad: What the Rich Teach Their Kids About Money That the Poor and Middle Class Do Not!* (Plata Publishing, 2022).

Livingston, Gretchen. "Four-in-Ten Couples are Saying 'I Do,' Again," Pew Research Center, November 14, 2014, last accessed June 13, 2025, https://www.pewresearch.org/social-trends/2014/11/14/chapter-2-the-demographics-of-remarriage/.

Rudnitsky, Matt. *You Are An Author: So Write Your Book Already* (Platypus Publications, 2016).

Stanbury, Caroline. "Why Marriage Doesn't Work for Women! With special guest Dr. Venus Nicolino." *Uncut and Uncensored with Caroline Stanbury*, episode 99. Dear Media, July 6, 2022. Podcast audio, 46 minutes. https://podcasts.apple.com/cy/podcast/why-

marriage-doesnt-work-for-women-with-special-
        guest/id1524317541?i=1000568977776.

"U.S. men die nearly six years before women, as life
        expectancy gap widens," Harvard T.H. Chan School
        of Public Health, November 13, 2023, last accessed
        June 13, 2025, https://hsph.harvard.edu/news/u-s-
        men-die-nearly-six-years-before-women-as-life-
        expectancy-gap-widens/.

Walsch, Neale Donalde. *Conversations with God: An
        Uncommon Dialogue* (G.P. Putnam's Sons, 1996).

William, Anthony. *Life-Changing Foods: Save Yourself and
        the Ones You Love with the Hidden Healing Powers of
        Fruits & Vegetables* (Hay House LLC, 2016).